A Professor's Diary

The Untold Story of Higher Education

Yuvaan
books
An Imprint of Unbound Script

A Professor's Diary
Written *by* Dr. Laxman Yadav
Translated *by* Reenu Talwar

ISBN : 978-81-19745-75-3

First Edition : Sep., 2024

Publisher : Unbound Script
2/41, Ansari Road
Daryaganj, Delhi-110002
Website : www.unboundscript.com
E-mail : books@unboundscript.com
Phone : 011-35807601

Printer : Yash Printographics
Noida, Uttar Pradesh

Price : ₹ 350/-

A Professor's Diary

The Untold Story of Higher Education

Dr. Laxman Yadav

Translated *by* Reenu Talwar

Yuvaan
books

For

Rohith Vemula

and those innumerable possibilities

that remained unfulfilled like him

A teacher who is himself afraid will teach his students to be spineless. These students will go on to become lifeless citizens of society.

Preface

The pen and books are humanity's unparalleled achievements. If labouring hands have shaped the world, those holding pens have filled it with colour. The vibrant culture we call India was crafted by farmers, labourers, artisans, and intellectuals over thousands of years. Intellectuals come from the farmer-labourer classes and ultimately speak for them. This image of India that we try to portray, as a 'Vishwaguru', a global guru, who created it? History may overlook it, but this culture was built by the farmer-labourer class that was always in the majority. Who were the creators of our vast folk literature? Who built the temples? Who were the people who carved beautiful sculptures? Who created unique carvings from clay and wood? Who were the royal artisans who built palaces and thrones? Who crafted attractive jewellery? Who built everything from roads to the pillars of the Parliament?

It is we who have filled in all the colours there are, in this image of Vishwaguru. And what is the actual plight of gurus In this country? And how much is the share of farmers, labourers, artisans, and marginalised communities among these gurus? Have we been able to open the doors of our schools, colleges, and universities for everyone? Does every hand have a book and a pen in it? Are our country's esteemed educational institutions still worthy of pride? To have an honest conversation about these questions is to do justice to the idea of Vishwguru.

Honesty demands that we not see only as much truth as those in power want to show us. To be an aware citizen, you must confront the truth that is hidden from you. The truth that is often not spoken about and is only endured. History is usually written in favour of the government and thus is never exhaustive. The stories of marginalised communities are often ignored in the narrative of history. But a time comes when those rejected by history come forward with their untold stories. In the words of Chinua Achebe, 'Until the deer don't themselves write their history, the history of deer will sing paeans of the hunters' bravery."

Amidst claims of India being a Vishwaguru, this book tells the truth about gurus and academic institutions, especially universities. This is a story of the academic world, seen from the perspective of an ad hoc professor. I kept writing down my experiences of almost two decades of academic life, sometimes in a notebook, sometimes in the empty pages of a book. I noted dates, recorded events I witnessed, preserved some heart-wrenching moments and jotted down some humorous incidents. People like us, who come from the first generation of Dalit-Bahujan communities, have countless such experiences in academic life. As time passed, I collected these scattered notes and comments into a book. This is my personal history, written from the heart.

This book contains the everyday experiences of countless temporary teachers working in universities and schools. These temporary teachers are known by many names such as ad hoc professors, guest lecturers, education friends, appointed teachers, and contract teachers. This book is the shared story of these different terms, whose job is the same - to study and to teach. A profession where everything is permanent except, of course, the teacher. The syllabus, students, studies, notes, chalk, duster, marker, building, events, duty usage – everything is permanent; but the teacher, at the centre of all these, is not permanent.

The education system of our country is, as if, on a ventilator today. Oxygen is being supplied to it through temporary teachers. I was an ad-hoc assistant professor at a prestigious central university in the capital of our country for almost fourteen years. It is risky to talk about what I saw. It has become our destiny to remain a part of the 'crowd'. I refused to be a part of the crowd therefore this book came to be in your hands. I want to take this risk knowing full well that the difficulties will increase after this. But the future of our children is at stake, hence there is no choice.

When a large number of children from Dalit, backward, tribal, pasmanda, and deprived sections began reaching institutions of higher education for the first time, the system started destroying them deliberately. A bright future is created with a pen and a book. Only when your children receive a good education will they be able to give you a better tomorrow. When they go to schools, colleges, and universities, they will understand many things and ask questions. They will learn and learn to fight too. That's why universities are being diminished in stature so that the politics of religious places remains strong. When universities are no longer the focal point, the conspiracy to involve young people in temples and mosques will be successful. When we should be concerned about opening new universities, new religious places are being built.

More than half of the teaching positions are vacant in almost all academic institutions in the country. Among these, more than ninety per cent of the reserved category posts don't have permanent appointments. You must have seen the deplorable condition of government schools in your village or town or nearby areas. The state of universities and degree colleges is no better. Except for a few central universities and degree colleges, government educational institutions in India are going through their worst phase. Most of them neither have buildings nor teachers. Everything is fine but it exists only on paper. The buildings exist on paper, teachers are on paper, education is on paper, and degrees are distributed on paper. You would know the tragic story of the opening and shutting down of numerous B.Ed. and engineering colleges. While reading this think of the government schools, degree colleges, and universities around you.

The scope of education is vast, it spreads from family to school and college to university. This book doesn't claim to lay before you the complete truth of the education world. It is the truth that I have personally experienced. Every temporary teacher's story won't be the same. Some female teacher's stories may turn out to be more tragic. The misfortune of a first-generation temporary teacher who comes from a deprived and exploited background could be more horrific. This book was written amid all the facilities available in the capital city of Delhi. The stories of temporary teachers struggling with worse difficulties in villages and towns would be much more terrible than my story.

In this era, one has to pay the price for speaking out. The powers that be are afraid of questions. They want to weaken the places that give us the strength to ask questions. That's why the authorities want the teachers to always live in fear.

A teacher who is afraid himself will teach his students to be spineless. These students will go on to become lifeless citizens of society.

The national media has lost its credibility among the common people. Does it express its concerns about education in the news anymore? Universities are news only when their buildings collapse or when the police use tear gas and batons on the campuses. When newspapers and journalists have been unable to save their conscience, how can they save education and teachers?

As you read this book, you will feel the passing of days, months, and years. Many years have been condensed into months and months into a few days. As you read, you won't even notice how the years passed. But when we were living it, each moment was a realisation. In this diary, the names of most institutions and individuals have been changed. This is not due to any fear or apprehension. It has been done so that instead of controversy or sensationalism, people can focus their attention on the core issues and concerns.

Today it is January 3rd, the birthday of Shiksha-Jyoti Savitribai Phule. I pay my respects to her memory. I am happy and content to have completed this book on this day. I am grateful to my friends who helped compile my diary entries, notes, and comments. I thank my editor and publisher for transforming it into a well-organised and beautiful book.

Dr. Laxman Yadav
January 3, 2024

To My Readers

When 'A Professor's Diary' came out in Hindi, it broke many records. Thirty-five thousand copies of it were sold in just one and a half months. Congratulatory messages came from countless people in different parts of the country. Some praised the book and had tears in their eyes, others said they could identify with the stories in the book, it was as if their story had been written. Thanks everyone.

I am proud to share with you that 'A Professor's Diary' has so far been published in four languages. After selling a record number of copies in Hindi, its Marathi and Punjabi versions have also come out.

We hope that the English translation will get the same love from you all.

Dr. Laxman Yadav
Mandal Jyanti
August 25, 2024

We listened to the UNTOLD STORIES of this world of dreams where we had arrived to make a place for ourselves.

August 2010

How it all began

A rainy evening. The fresh scent of wet earth, soaked by showers, is wafting all around. It's been over a year since I came to Delhi but the smell of damp earth still pleases me. The rows of Neem, Champa and Saptaparni trees, adorned with rain-washed leaves, seem like sentinels working overtime. Ajay and I are going from the North Campus to Hudson Lane on foot, to meet Raghu Da. Many friends have advised me to start looking for an ad hoc job while doing my PhD.

'Ad hoc'! These words hit me with a particular seriousness, especially in this season.

I had no idea what 'Ad Hoc' really was till the advice of two friends piqued my curiosity. Therefore I talked to Ajay. We decided to go to the campus in the evening as Raghu da was the right person to discuss it with. At this stage in my academic life, much thought was going into the pros and cons of this decision. Hence, we reached the North Campus of Delhi University to meet Raghu da with many conflicting thoughts in my head. When we arrived, before I could open my mouth, Ajay said:

"Raghu da, Laxman needs to discuss 'ad hoc' with you."

"So tell me, Laxman, what are you thinking?"

"Yesterday I went for an interview at Jhalkari Bai College. The board asked me a few strange questions and then dismissed me saying that I was still a kid and should focus on my studies. I am thinking seriously about it now. But I don't have much information, therefore we came over to know your take on it. What is this ad hoc all about?

I was feeling uncomfortable actually. Till yesterday, I was a student and today I wanted to become a teacher. The thought was giving me goosebumps. Having closely observed many of my fine teachers and wonderful professors, the desire to teach had always been there in some corner of my heart. But how would that come about? I was, of course, familiar with the complicated world of books, ideas and principles but this new path, leading towards teaching, was still unexplored. Given his vast experience, Raghu da began to elucidate my confused state of mind as he would the nuances of a poem.

"You know, Laxman, every year the rainy season brings the chance of becoming an ad hoc professor. The many colleges of DU are like fertile fields for those seeking a teaching career. Thousands of posts are vacated each year in these colleges, many professors take leave for various reasons and temporary assistant professors are chosen to take their place. These teachers, employed for a few months, are known as 'ad hoc' here. People say that once employed as 'ad hoc', it won't be long till you get a permanent position. If that is what you want, go for it. However, you should know that not everyone who sets out can attain this goal."

We have spent many hours of 'Satsang', which loosely translated into English means a kind of communion with truth, with Raghu da, soaking up so much knowledge. He knows how to look at everything with a perspective. He has the aura of a spiritual teacher. This communion with truth is the real thing to be learnt, relevant even when it is not found in any academic curriculum or as we say here, it is 'out of syllabus'. Today when Raghu da likened being an ad hoc teacher to being in love, I willingly allowed myself to go deep into that thought. God knows what Ajay understood, but allegorising ad hoc to falling in love had touched me. As if, being an ad hoc teacher was also an altogether different and beautiful feeling like being in love. So what if it was difficult? For people like us, falling in love hasn't been easy either!

This was my first informal lesson to make sense of the academic world which would begin on the lawn near the library in the North Campus and get adjourned at the tea stall. Such lessons are not meant to end. Right now, the guru is in his element, his experiences flowing intuitively in his words. "Spontaneous overflow of powerful emotions." He speaks as if to introduce us to the beauty of Wordsworth's romantic poems –

"As far as professorship is concerned, DU is like a huge farm. If there is a farm, there has to be a landlord, a moneylender, a farmer, and bonded labour. The syllabus to be taught is the seed and fertiliser. The size of the field hasn't increased but, over time, the number of people depending on it has increased considerably. Everyone wants a piece of it. Everyone is in a rush - some helping others, some pushing others out of the way. With the desire to become a professor, people start going from college to college during the rainy season. Now you too wish to join them. Good. You must try."

Raghu Da aka Raghuvir Prasad is from Ghazipur in U.P. He is well-known in the Hindi academic circles. Since his JNU days, so many people must have sought his help for anything from writing a synopsis to submitting a PhD thesis. While he knew his subject extremely well, he barely knew the workings of the academic world that would help him obtain a permanent post as a professor. Raghu da is an extraordinary person. He did his BA from Allahabad University, his MA from BHU and his PhD from JNU. After finishing his research at JNU, he had to leave the campus but could not bear being far away from his beloved university, therefore he began living in neighbouring Munirka.

Now and then, he would get an ad hoc post or teach as a guest lecturer in some college. After a few days, he began living temporarily in Sant Nagar, Burari, near the North Campus. One of his relatives lives there and does tailoring work. Living with him, Raghu da would occasionally do some stitching and hemming, just for fun, not under any compulsion. He was fascinated by the needle and thread. He would often say:

"The world is in tatters. We can save it one stitch at a time. The academic world teaches us to repair our fraying dreams, like a tailor. The pen is the needle that mends civilisation."

Once Raghu da mentioned that he missed Sudesh Mahto a lot. Sudesh was the topper of their batch. He had published two books and many articles. They had come to Delhi together. It was a big thing to progress from a backward area in Jharkhand, where there were barely any roads, to the smooth expressways of Delhi. They had become friends at BHU. Having got a chance to be in JNU, they boarded the train of dreams and got off at Delhi, the city of hope. For us, a professor was the very backbone of society, who helped produce people with spines who had strength and fortitude. But we observed that people here instead of standing tall, were reduced to crawling and lacked the backbone to hold them upright. Sudesh was a very sincere person. To him, none of this felt quite right. God alone knows why and where to he disappeared one day. The successful ones are often feted here, in various gatherings, but this campus seldom gives a thought to those who have returned home or have just disappeared.

Sitting on the DU campus, this was the first lesson that made us aware of the inside reality of the academic world. We listened to the untold stories of this world of dreams where we had arrived to make a place for ourselves. Raghu da had himself taught as an ad hoc professor in many colleges. But these days he was unemployed. "So where is the interview?", Raghu Da asked. I replied, "Maulana Azad Delhi Callege." Raghu da immediately said:

"Great! But it is a College, not Callege. It is a 300-year-old educational institution, one of the oldest in Asia. I taught there as a guest lecturer for four months. This College, standing in the heart of Delhi used to be a Madarsa, once upon a time. Later it became Delhi College, a centre for education in Science and Literature. It has witnessed all the events that happened between 1857 and 1947. Its library somehow managed to escape being burnt down. Recently there have been some good recruitments there. You must go."

After downing the second cup of tea, we prepared to leave. We took an autorickshaw from The GTB Nagar traffic lights to Mukherjee Nagar. My interest had grown in leaps and bounds. Ajay had appeared for three interviews for ad hoc positions and as a senior, he tried to counsel me,

"Don't feel stressed, yaar. Whatever is best for you, will happen. Surely, one day we too will be permanent professors at DU."

I reached my room. Before falling asleep, I gave myself a pep talk, what was the harm in trying one more time? We had decided to meet at 10 a.m, at the callege itself.

Oh, I meant to say COLLEGE.

Like a farmer, who gives his all in the hope of a bountiful crop, I too came back full of optimism. A farmer and an unemployed person both are aware that it isn't given that there will be a bumper crop each time. But who can stop hope from filling one's heart?

31st August 2010

A Knock On The Door

I reached the college for my interview at the scheduled time. And I found out that all my friends had ditched me. Ajay called and said he had something important to attend to, therefore he was unable to come. Mahesh didn't take my call. Vimal began telling me over the phone how disheartened he was after appearing for so many interviews. "This is just your second interview, go for it". I felt alone and abandoned. I thought I should just go back. Then again I felt, now that I was there, what was the harm in appearing for the interview? Whatever will be, will be. We'll see later.

I sat in front of the Principal's office and waited for my turn. While my gaze was fixed on the door, my mind was a churn of unpalatable thoughts. I was upset with my friends for not showing up to support me. Just then, the person sitting next to me asked:

"Your name?"

"Laxman, and yours?"

"Dr. Mohammad Shakir. Where are you from?"

"I am doing PhD at DU itself, and you?"

'I am from AMU, Aligarh. Since you are from here, you must know how things work, and what the situation looks like. How many interviews have you appeared for till now?

'I don't know much about the situation. This is my second interview. And yours?

The person smiled and said:

"Don't even ask. I have appeared for so many interviews that I have become used to it now. I have taught everywhere, in Degree colleges and even in schools. It seems my whole life will pass like this, appearing for interviews. I am from a farming background and I dreamed of becoming a professor. And on top of that…anyway, leave it be."

Yesterday Raghu da too had said almost the same thing about interviews. In my mind, it felt as if it was cloudy and sunny at the same time. Just then, another candidate came in, Sukesh Kumar, who was my super-senior and was known to Shakir. In a philosophical tone, he said:

"Shakir bhai, in reality, these interviews are a sham. Even before the they begin, the result is already decided. People in big posts decide among themselves that 'A' should be placed here and 'B', we will see about later. They don't want to let people like us know that. They ask mock questions and pretend to listen to our responses. They make sure that they don't accidentally smile at our helplessness. It is all a sham, bhai."

I was appearing for the second interview of my academic life and I was getting to hear all this. Shakir told me that Sukesh had appeared for three dozen interviews till now. He got a chance to teach two or three times but soon fell prey to academic politics. Whereas Sukesh continued to vent the resentment behind his vast yet unfruitful academic experience.

"For most interviews, the result is decided way before the given date. The Principal, teacher-in-charge or whoever is seniormost have already made the decision and it is only left to be announced. External forces play a part too in this decision. Every professor has a heart that beats for his family, caste, language, region, party or ideology. Barely five to ten people are selected based on the interview.

For us, caste identity is like paracetamol. In politics, from Principals to Prime Ministers, everyone liberally uses this drug."

I was in a difficult situation. Why did I even come for the interview without getting someone to advocate my candidacy? I should have talked to someone about it. But to whom? The atmosphere around me was becoming increasingly unbearable. There were many people here who had written and published as much as two times their body weight and they were three times my age. So what did I have to lose? Just then my name was called.

The interview began, after the introductions, questions were asked about my PhD. The board members kept up the questions and I answered with all my heart. A senior board member, a lady began showing appreciation for my replies after the third or fourth response and kept saying "That's good. Very good." This was enough to boost my confidence. Out of the eight or ten questions, I could not answer two and apologised for not being able to reply. Then, the principal, sitting on the chair opposite me began asking the questions.

"You are from Azamgarh, so why did you go to Allahabad to study? Isn't there a college in Azamgarh?"

"Sir, merely having a college building doesn't necessarily ensure that education is being imparted. There has to be an atmosphere of learning. The atmosphere at Allahabad University is not to be found in any college in my district." The principal asked me some questions about the interrelation of school and higher education. Then about my favourite poet and poem. In the end, he asked,

'If we choose you, what will you do for our college that is new and different?'

This question somehow filled me with hope. I don't exactly remember my reply, but I remember he had a look of approval on his face. After the interview, which lasted around ten minutes, I came out and ran into Mohammad Shakir from Aligarh. He asked me how it went and the questions that were asked. I don't much recall what I told him either. Before leaving, I enquired from the office, "When will the result be out and how will we come to know?" They said, "Those who are selected will get a call by this evening."

Like a farmer, who gives his all in the hope of a bountiful crop, I too came back full of optimism. A farmer and an unemployed person both are aware that it isn't given that there will be a bumper crop each time. But who can stop hope from filling one's heart?

It took a long time for evening to come, that day. And when it did arrive, it was in a hurry to get over. But no phone call had come. It became dark. Around six thirty pm, the mobile phone rang. A voice asked, "Is this Mr. Laxman? You had come for an interview at Maulana Azad Delhi College?"

"Yes, I did."

"You have been selected. Please come at 10 a.m. tomorrow with your original documents."

It is difficult to explain how important that phone call was for me. I was beside myself with happiness. I thought perhaps I shouldn't share the news with my family just yet. "Let us wait and see what happens in college tomorrow. Let me join first, then I will break the news at home," I thought. But I couldn't stop myself from calling Amma and sharing the news with her.

It was impossible to sleep that night. I began thinking of my identity, of my Amma, Papa, my uncle, my sisters, my brother, my grandmother and grandfather, my great grandfather…I thought of everyone I could recall. For the very first time, someone from their family was about to become a professor. So many generations who had grazed cows and goats in blazing afternoons when hot loo winds blew, who had got drenched in the rain as they transplanted paddy and weeded the fields, who had woken up at midnight in the dead of winter to water the wheat fields and who lived and died doing just that…Perhaps, they had never had such lofty dreams. Carpenters, barbers, cobblers, tailors, potters, blacksmiths, weavers, cowherds, boatmen and sweepers had neither any land to their name nor the luxury of dreaming. From centuries their children had continually been buried in the very foundations of civilisation. The eyes that could read the sky for signs of changing weather, could also foresee the bleak future of farming and physical labour. Therefore, they saved each rupee to send their children to school. They began to understand that only education could break the chains of this centuries-old slavery. Jyotiba Phule, Savitribai Phule, Fatima Sheikh, Periyar, Shahuji, Bhagat Singh and Dr. Ambedkar, who helped build our nation were a little late in understanding this.

We got the opportunity to get out of farms and barns and into schools. We are indebted to the centuries of sweat, toil and labour by our ancestors. Education enables us to repay that debt. When a young person of this generation becomes a teacher, he writes a new chapter of civilisation. God knows why, but tonight, I will sleep with a pen in my hand.

The individuals responsible for weakening these esteemed universities are typically those who oppose opportunities being given to the deprived and underprivileged of the society.

1st September 2010

Making a Nest on the Tree

It is a new morning today. There have hardly been any such luminous mornings in these twenty-one years. So many generations lived and worked in darkness in order that we could see the light of this day. We had faith that such a day would surely dawn. Before every big exam or even a test, I always talk to Amma. I called Amma today too, for I was going to join a new job, that of an ad hoc professor. This too was an exam, in a way, of a kind.

I reached Maulana Azad Delhi College for the joining. Mirza Ghalib was supposed to come and teach in this college. When he reached the gate of the college, he saw that the head of the institution had not come out to receive him. He was offended and he left. Anyway, there was no one like Mirza Ghalib. What was this world of teaching and professorship before him! Yes, it was the same college, and here was I standing in front of it – a twenty-one-and-a-half-year-old novice. I quietly walked through the gates of Delhi College, all alone.

I ran into Shakir bhai. Yes, the same Mohammad Shakir who I had met on the day of the interview. I asked him:

"Shakir bhai, how come you are here?"

"I have been selected as a guest lecturer, and you?"

"Ad hoc."

"Great! Strange is life, we had to eventually work together, that is why we met each other on the day of the interview. Come, let us get on with the joining formalities."

We joined the college together. He hurried on towards the staffroom and I stood in front of the office staring at the imposing building of the college. I had never seen such a grand government college till now. Most of the government schools and colleges in our district are nothing more than ruins where stray cattle and abandoned dreams take refuge. India's future is being forged in those ruins. God knows what kind of future it will be and of which India?

I had felt this sense of awe before during my PhD admission to the North Campus of Delhi University. No doubt, academic buildings don't contribute much to the future of the students who study there; but what of the generations of students who are being educated without classrooms, buildings and teachers? They would have some kind of future too, no?

Even today, Allahabad University is so beloved to people like me. That university made us what we are today. From my village, I had brought the dreams of the generations that had gone before me and placed them on the historical dome and minarets of the Senate Hall.

I was so sure that the realisation of those dreams would begin there. Allahabad University gave wings to my dreams. And thus I landed at Delhi University. With time my dreams grew bigger. They had learnt how to fly at Allahabad University and today, here they were, perched on the lofty and historical walls of Maulana Azad Delhi College.

You have to ask people like me what value a centralised university holds for us, because that is where we came into our own. That is why it is most painful for us when cracks appear in them. The individuals responsible for weakening these esteemed universities are typically those who oppose opportunities being given to the deprived and underprivileged of the society. Actually, education is an eyesore for the powers that be in every era. Education empowers the new generations to ask questions. It was a complete education that I received at Allahabad University, not just a degree. I therefore understand that preserving such educational establishments is essentially about preserving future generations.

'Quot Rami tot Arbores', As many branches, so many trees is the motto of Allahabad University. We are the branches of that university. Universities are the foundation of our civilisation. Why would a civilised society do something to weaken its very foundation?

I received the joining letter stating that the job is only for four months. I did not have any clue how dangerous this four-month game would turn out to be.

I gazed at the joining letter for a long time. Underneath my name, it was written - Assistant Professor. At that moment, I was beginning to recognise my identity in a new way. The last time this had happened was when I qualified for the Junior Research Fellowship. Uncle was overjoyed for me, and also because I would no longer be relying on him to send me money every month.

He had ensured that I continued my studies by spending way above and beyond his resources, so why wouldn't he be happy? What if Uncle hadn't been there? My father, a poor man, could have offered me only two things, which he gave freely; composure and courage. These degrees meant nothing to him. He was an idealist and a socialist.

That day, it was my Amma who was the happiest. But she lovingly reproached me in Bhojpuri.

"Very good that you did JRF. But if you had done B. Ed, you would have become a teacher in a primary school by now."

My mother belonged to a generation when it wasn't difficult to become a primary school teacher after completing a Bachelor of Education degree (B.Ed). Until then, B. Ed colleges hadn't mushroomed everywhere and hadn't become businesses handing out degrees for a hefty fee. Despite several attempts, she had been unable to complete her B. Ed. Now she is an Anganwadi worker. She had a suppressed desire to become a teacher. She did not know what it meant to pass the Net-JRF exam and become a professor. Papa and one of my uncles knew that after getting a JRF and doing PhD, it was possible to be appointed as a professor. Therefore they were happy about it. But nothing could beat Amma's happiness. She could not become a teacher herself, but she had created me with her aborted dreams. Her son had become a professor today.

Meanwhile, a tear drop fell on the joining letter, startling me out of my thoughts. I pulled myself together, wiped it off and moved on.

I reached the staff room. I learned there that the department head is known as the 'Teacher In-Charge,' or TIC. Dr. Suresh Saxena, was part of the interview board, therefore I recognized him and he recognized me. Upon seeing me, he raised his hand in a blessing. I mean, I only bowed a bit out of respect, maybe under the influence of the Allahabad feudal tradition, and he generously made a gesture to bless me. We harbour a great misconception that 'small' cities like Allahabad, Banaras, and Patna are the only places where feudalism exists. Not even the so-called educated people can overcome this deeply ingrained casteism, regionalism, feudalism and patriarchy. They plant the same old seeds everywhere they go, which results in thriving of egos and frustration. Saxena sir introduced me to the rest of the teachers in the department. It turned out that I was the only ad hoc teacher in this department, at the moment. The two people who were ad hoc before me had become permanent last month. Saxena sir said:

"Mr. Laxman! Whoever comes here, remains here forever. I am quite sure that it will be you who becomes permanent next."

When I heard him say this, I felt deep hope and determination. After all, we nurture our dreams on the fertile ground of hope, don't we? Among those whom Saxena sir introduced me to was Dr. Jitendra Singh. Smiling in response to my greeting, Dr. Jitendra Singh shook my hand. He didn't try at all to bless me. Spontaneously, I said, "Thank you, sir." He replied, "Not sir, call me Jitendra. It would be nice if you address me by my name."

I felt I could straighten my spine and stand tall, after hearing him say that. Undoubtedly, it was thought to be polite to literally prostrate oneself at the lotus-feet of elders and seniors. Professors such as Satyaprakash Mishra sir, who would become agitated and reprimand others if they tried to touch his feet, were powerless to change the age-old tradition on their own. Where I come from, shaking hands with someone older than you was considered disrespectful.

However, professors Rajender Kumar and Pranay Krishna of the same Allahabad University, had laid the foundation of having a smart mind, a tongue that asks questions and a straight spine for standing tall. All of that had come with me.

Jitendra sir and Shabina ma'am had been the ad hoc teachers in the Hindi department before me. Over time, I discovered that the ad hocs handle the majority of the paperwork for the timetable, college, and department. Ad hoc professors are not permitted to do one thing though, they cannot sign any document. Mohammad Shakir and I began to get involved with the paperwork.

Saxena sir gave me the timetable. For a new professor, this was a significant moment. The last time I had felt such joy was when I became the topper of the M.A. program and a gold medalist of my batch at Allahabad University and had received my M.A. mark sheet from the senior clerk of the Hindi department. I felt exactly the same way today when I took the timetable from Saxena sir, as I did when I had taken my mark sheet from the hands of the clerk. Now I was an Assistant Professor at DU. I was looking forward to my classes. But they were scheduled for tomorrow, not today. That is, the teaching would begin from tomorrow.

Shakir bhai left for Aligarh. He would return with wife, kids, bags and baggage. After long, he too had found a place to settle down. On my way back, I went to the campus. Raghu Da came out from the library and we went to have tea. Lighting his cigarette, he asked,

"So tell me ad hoc professor Laxman, how was your first day at college?"

I became a little emotional and said, "I have just started writing a new chapter in the book of my life, Dada. Of course, I am happy, but I'm feeling uncomfortable about one thing. The phone calls that came to congratulate me would end with this question, "Who recommended you? Who put in a good word? How did you get the job?"

Understanding my predicament, Raghu da said, "It is common here. After someone gets a job, there are always rumours that they had a strong recommendation from some important person. And there is a reason behind all this. You can't give any credible reply to such rumours. Even if you do, it won't make any difference. In the eyes of the world, a professor's job is obtained through degrees, capabilities, and merit. Behind the scenes, everyone knows that without connections, no one can get it just like that. Therefore, your ad hoc appointment will always be suspect in their eyes. Don't worry too much about it. You must take this excellent beginning to its logical conclusion."

I returned from the campus to my room, feeling a bit relieved. Although a doubt still niggled. I had come to Delhi to become an IAS officer. The line 'We should change the system, from within the system' was pasted on the wall next to my timetable right in front of the study table, since my graduation days. Also, since my childhood, Papa would always say, "My son will become a Collector one day." I too began to feel that I was born on this earth to bring about a radical transformation. What change could I bring about as a professor? I've got a fellowship, and an opportunity to pursue a PhD from a prestigious university like DU. I also felt that I wouldn't have made it this far if some of my professors hadn't been good. I owe them a great deal.

My uncle, who I called 'bade pitaji', once told me that although altering the course of a nation wasn't an easy task, changing the course of the next generation was a much more difficult one. A teacher is a guru; he has far more authority and significance. A professor contributes immensely to the transformation of the future generations. My dilemma was still not resolved.

On the other hand, when the villagers and relatives came to know about my appointment, my uncle Khedaran taunted my father one day, saying:

"Shivnarayan Babu! All else is fine, but had your son become a collector, his photo would have been published in the newspaper. The entire district would have known that so-and-so's son had made a name for himself. A professor has no extra income, no power, no prestige. What's the use of being a professor nowadays? And that too, a professor of Hindi!"

My family is overjoyed. They don't realise that I'm about to embark on a never-ending game that requires constant play, days, weeks, and years at a time. The rules of the game would occasionally change in the middle of a round, and occasionally the players would change too. At that moment, my uncle, my bade pitaji called and said:

"Yesterday you had mentioned that you wanted to buy a motorcycle, I've sent the money. Don't ever say that you will pay me back from your salary. What all will you pay us back? Keep this one thing in mind, you should know how to spend money before you have any. Buy a good motorbike for yourself and ride carefully."

The mirrors stayed the same, but my REFLECTIONS changed with time.

2nd September 2010

A Professor in the Mirror

I will take my first class today. As a teacher, I'm using the same bag that I used when I was a student. I am ready with a notebook, notes from my MA and JRF days, and a pen. Before leaving, I stood in front of the mirror. As a child, I used to secretly look at my reflection in the mirror, always trying to find someone else's face in my own. I grew older and outgrew all that. But God alone knows why, at this moment, I can see the faces of my forefathers in this mirror. The mirror has somehow always put me to the test. Every time I look into it, I experience both intense terror and extreme self-confidence. The mirrors stayed the same, but my reflections changed with time. I feel as if the mirror is questioning me today, "Are you really an Assistant Professor? An Assistant Professor at Delhi University?"

As always, I left without answering the mirror's question. According to the timetable, I will teach Bhakti poetry to first-year Hindi honours students today. I will share two classes with the department's most senior professor, Arora Ma'am. I reached the class and had barely started speaking-

"My name is Laxman, and today, I will teach you about Kabir."

A voice came from behind:

"Show us your ID card first, then we'll believe you."

Suddenly, it felt as if the mirror in my room had followed me to the classroom. I had no idea the mirror would permanently hang on the wall opposite me in every class, and that it would test me every time I taught. In this day and age of masked faces, it is so difficult to face this mirror test. Keeping calm, I replied,

"I am your new professor. From now on, I will teach you Bhakti poetry."

"There is a ban on ragging in this college. How can we believe that you are our professor? Please show us your ID card."

It was a valid question. But I didn't have any solid evidence to show. I hadn't received any identity card or badge. And professors don't have a uniform, anyway. But in the next few minutes, I managed to convince them with my words that even though I may not look the part or seem old enough, I was indeed their professor. That student apologized later.

A temporarily employed person like me is constantly trying to convince himself and everyone else about his credentials, each moment, everywhere.

The first class began with a round of introductions. I told the students about myself, asked them about themselves. I wanted to cherish that moment. I used to see my favourite professors standing in the place where I was standing today. I thought about many of my teachers, OP sir, KP sir from school, professors Satyaprakash Mishra, Rajendra Kumar, Pranay Krishna, Nisha Agarwal, Ramkishore, Dr. Lalasa ma'am, and Dr. Mustaq Ali from Allahabad University. I was living whatever I had learned from them, about Hindi and also about life. My dream of becoming a professor, which I had while I was their student, was beginning to come true today.

After the introductions, we discussed the syllabus and books. The bell rang at its scheduled time. The first class came to an end. As I returned to the staffroom after teaching my first class, I felt a unique sense of accomplishment. It was as if my feet were drunk on the success of reaching the destination after an endless journey.

There was another class after an hour. I had to teach students of the B.A program. There too, we went from introductions to discussing the syllabus and books, and the class got over. In the college and classroom, not for a moment did I feel that I was a temporary professor. The college was outstanding. I continued to take in its splendour and also carried it back with me. When I called my friend that night, I felt so overwhelmed.

You know, with a pen and a book I am writing a new chapter in my life. Today, it felt how a landless labourer would feel if he gets a piece of land. I've returned home after staring at that field with satisfaction and daydreaming about the endless possibilities of its harvest. Not all persons of my age have access to such opportunities. Countless young people are forced to return home after taking the several exams that are a part of the current system. I got the opportunity to become a professor. My batchmates, Rakesh, Sangeeta, Manoj, Abhinav, Renu, and Phoolbadan, must be engaged in farming, doing manual labour or cooking and washing dishes in the village. And here I am, back home after teaching at a college in Delhi University. I am missing them a lot."

"This is the problem with you, you get too emotional too soon."

There must be exceptions too, but how many?

27th September 2010

Tales from the staffroom

There's a freshers' party for first-year students in the college today. Each program in the college is a new experience for me. During these initial days, whenever I saw the number of opportunities the students of my college had or when I watched college events, I thought of the young people of my village. Students studying in each college of Delhi University have access to the debating society, theatre society, dance and music society, NCC, NSS, judo, karate, table tennis, chess, basketball, hockey, football, cricket, and many other sports societies. Students join these societies according to their choice and capabilities.

I have seen many government degree colleges and campuses from Azamgarh to Allahabad, but none had such facilities. To wish for such extracurricular activities to take place there is like expecting barren land to grow lush crops. The countless young people of this country have no access to basic infrastructure like buildings, teachers, and classes. A farmer can turn unproductive land into fertile ground with his hard work, but he cannot ensure quality education for his children with his labour. If he wants his child to study, where should he send them? In those parts of the country, nothing is available.

I couldn't help thinking that in this country, we also have some government colleges that take six years to award a three-year BA degree. Although everyone understands the importance of higher education in our country, it has been marginalised, much like an elderly person in a family, who has a wealth of experience to contribute but no one is prepared to listen. There must be exceptions too, but how many, I wonder.

At the freshers' party, students were sharing their experiences. While some liked the greenery of the college campus, others liked the book-filled library. Some were complaining about the samosas in the canteen, while others were unhappy about not getting their desired subject. But I was amazed to see that these young people were full of self-confidence. In our village, kids of this age are hesitant to even look you in the eye, let alone speak up. A boy came on stage and said:

"I like this college a lot. The professors are also good. Saxena sir talks to us very kindly. Arora ma'am is like a mother figure. Jitendra sir has an amazing way of teaching. Laxman sir makes everything easy for us to understand. I feel that I have begun a new life in this college."

I was surprised when the boy mentioned my name along with Saxena sir, Arora ma'am, and

Jitendra sir. I remember Raghu da had said that an ad hoc professor like me should never do their job so well that they are compared with a permanent professor. That is an unpardonable sin, and the punishment is meted out silently. After the program, Saxena sir said, "Laxman ji, I'm so glad the students have praised you too. Now I feel it was a good decision to choose you as an ad hoc professor. I have high expectations from you. All the best. I am sure you will become a permanent professor here, you have my blessing."

Upon hearing him say this, I felt that when people claim that ad hoc teachers are exploited, they exaggerate. This college is so good. Saxena sir and Arora ma'am have started respecting me. Raman Kumar sir, Mahendra sir, and Jitendra sir treat me as if I were a colleague of their age and share their stories and experiences from DU-JNU with me.

The staff room of Maulana Azad College slowly began to seem familiar. All the students at Delhi University aren't alike, but the ad hoc professors are. However, not all have colleagues as supportive as mine. I was thinking about this when I reached the Campus. At the gate of the Central Library, I ran into Shalini. Shalini had been my batchmate at Allahabad University. She too became an ad hoc professor at Dhanraj College that year. Just as I was about to excitedly share stories of our staff room with her, Shalini said in a rather frustrated tone,

"Yaar, an all-women college is like one's in-laws' house. The senior teachers there treat us ad hoc professors as if we were their newly arrived daughters-in-law and they, our mothers-in-law. They keep giving us instructions. 'Do this, do that, don't do this, sit here, why do you sit there, don't talk too much with Swati, why don't you bring lunch, you look better in salwar suits than in jeans, don't hobnob much with the students, haven't you found the book I had asked you to look for,' Khandelwal ma'am goes on and on like this. I'm so harassed. What should I do? She will be TIC for another two years."

Shalini's friend Aishwarya was also with her. She had been teaching in Phoolan Devi College for the last one and a half years. She too began recounting her experience, "Exactly! Shalini, what you said, about our college being like the in-laws' house for us, is one hundred per cent true. In my college, everyone isn't like that, only Priti and Malini ma'am behave like mother-in-law. They are seniormost, and we have no choice but to tolerate them. Allow some time to pass, slowly you'll get used to it. This is the story of every college, yaar. Don't take it so seriously."

I suppressed the desire to share how the staff room at Maulana Azad felt like paradise and kept listening to both of them quietly. Shalini had been working as an ad hoc professor for the past three months and she was full of anger as she continued to share her experience-

"All the ad hoc teachers listen to their discourse for hours on end. I'm so fed up. Just now, I invented an excuse that I had some urgent work in Kamla Nagar. Khandelwal ma'am scolded me, saying, 'Is there something more important than college for you?' I simply replied, 'Ma'am, all my classes are over for the day.' You tell me, Laxman, did I say anything wrong? Every day, Rekha travels with her in the metro to Jahangirpuri and then returns to Laxmi Nagar after she gets off. Mrs. Khandelwal thinks all ad hoc teachers should be as obedient as Rekha. It's unbearable. I had thought that as a professor I would have to teach students. I had no clue this job involved so much sycophancy. I can't do it. Aishwarya, I can't live like this. We have no dignity whatsoever."

Every temporary employee is brimming with so much discontent. All it takes is a little empathy and all their stories come pouring out. In two-three years of service alone, one is already so full of misgivings. A little while later, Shalini and Aishwarya went towards Gate Number 4 and disappeared from view. Just as all poor people aren't the same, all ad hoc teachers at Delhi University are not alike either. Just as one cannot fully understand a poor person's state of poverty without considering his caste, gender, region, etc., one cannot understand an ad hoc teacher without considering their temperament, the college environment, and the behaviour of the senior professors.

Being a professor seemed such a lofty idea. I used to believe that professors were people who gave direction to society. I have been fortunate to have many wonderful professors in my academic life. But there is a flip side to the coin, one that Shalini and Aishwarya talked about.

It is you who benefits if the backbone is straight, if it becomes flexible it is the system that benefits.

7th November 2010

Classrooms and Revolution

The initial few months of professorship passed in the novelty of this new life. The enthusiasm for taking classes was like adding a fresh page to the book of life daily. The best thing about doing a PhD is that you are not restricted by a syllabus anymore, you can read and write whatever interests you. As a result, books on various subjects jostled for space in my room. There were also notes from my MA, NET-JRF preparation days and the Delhi University syllabus. All this helped me prepare for my classes. When I taught a class, it was as if I was reliving what I had learned.

During every lecture, I would ask myself, 'Isn't this the perfect time to start bringing about a radical change in the future generation?' I would eventually conclude that perhaps it would be best to understand the system first. I would hear rumours that I could be thrown out of my job after four months. The threat of losing my job 'after four months' started to loom large over my plans to start a revolution. Inadvertently, I too started conforming to the system. Today, while teaching the interpretation of poetry in class, I came across a verse:

> leek leek sab koi chale, leekhin chale kapoot;
> leek chhod kar teen chalen, shayar soor sapoot.

Imagine what must be going through my mind while explaining this verse. With a gender-sensitive approach, it was critiqued for its patriarchal language because you'll find plenty of sons as 'saput-kaput' in literature, but daughters are absent. We continue living with this discrimination, not just in the cultural and social spheres, but in literature. Just then the bell rang, signalling the end of the period.

I had reached a compromise with the professor inside me who wished to bring about a radical change. While this compromise was a smart move as far as my profession was concerned, it was not good for my self-respect. If the backbone is perfectly straight, it causes excruciating pain when you bend it. It is you who benefits if the backbone is straight, if it becomes flexible it is the system that benefits. It is not desirable to be unbending, one of the conditions of success is the ability to be flexible. The spine stays taut like a bowstring as long as it is not compromised. When it becomes pliable, one blends into the system.

Whatever the era, there is no cure for delusions. We too were deluded into thinking we were assistant professors, but in reality, we were nothing more than professors on contract. Being temporary

✿ All follow the beaten path, even the worthless son
Three take a different one, poet, warrior, dutiful son

means one has to remain flexible. That's why things were being made temporary.

Hori, a character from Premchand's novel Godaan, lived and died with a desire to own a cow. Today's Hori lives with the desire for an ad hoc job and fights with his life to hang on to it. Let's see what is still to be accomplished in the life of a modern Hori. Even today he says,

"One should caress the foot that presses down on one's neck, that's the wise thing to do."

Contractual employees are forced to caress the feet that press down on their necks. Ad hoc assistant professors have no choice but to be obsequious towards powerful senior professors, principals, and Vice-Chancellors, to caress the feet that have weight. You understand what I mean by weight, don't you?

In a story by the famous writer Chekhov, a character who is a clerk dies worrying about whether his sneezing had offended the master in some way. Temporary employees have already 'sneezed' many times in front of their masters. That's why they worry, and die a little every day. Chekhov's clerk can be seen everywhere - in schools, offices, and companies - afraid of sneezing and dying a little every day.

Higher EDUCATION is no longer about subjects or ideas, it is about having the right c-o-n-n-e-c-t-i-o-n-s and manipulation.

15th November 2010

A Research Guide like him

These days, forms are being filled out for the permanent appointment of assistant professors at Delhi University. Many colleges are conducting interviews. Every other person is advising me to begin the efforts to secure a permanent position, I am an ad hoc employee. The convention at DU has been that those who become ad hoc have a higher chance of becoming permanent. Two ad hoc professors in my department became permanent in August. Currently, there are only about 700 to 800 ad hoc employees in DU.

This is the time when, after 2006, appointments began again at DU. It's been barely four months since I started working as an ad hoc. But acquaintances all around are filling out forms for permanent positions. I haven't completed my PhD yet, but I have the minimum eligibility criteria i.e. an M.A. degree and a NET-JRF. Technically I can become a permanent professor. Unable to decide what to do, I went to meet Rai sir on my way back from college.

Dr. Veershwar Rai sir is my supervisor. He is a professor of Hindi at Birsamunda College on the North Campus. Since I became an ad hoc professor, Rai sir has been very pleased with me. He had a lot of respect for me earlier too, but now he is even more content. He is considered one of the most popular Hindi teachers on the campus. His proficiency in language and excellent communication skills add another dimension to his calm and serious personality. He has such a strong grasp of modern poetry that even his casual conversations are like poetic compositions replete with symbols and motifs. All in all, he has an extremely aware, sensitive, and gentle personality. Rai sir came out after taking a class, enquired how I had been, and discussed my PhD work. After a while, he said, "Come, Laxman! Let's have lunch."

At a time when many of my researcher friends find their supervisors very distant and have a strained relationship with them, Rai sir is sharing his lunch with me. After being taught by a professor, at college or university, we have a research supervisor for PhD. Research scholars discuss various topics with them in depth. Research is the most appealing and essential part of higher education. Higher education is responsible for developing new ideas, new critiques, new languages, and new perspectives in any society.

Rai sir is such a research supervisor. I realised the importance of a research supervisor when I saw my friends being humiliated and insulted by their supervisors. I took the first bite of roti from the tiffin, and Sir said, "Tell me, Laxman, how's your teaching work going? What have you been teaching?"

"It's been a great experience, Sir. I'm teaching Bhakti poetry in the honours program and Hindi A in the BA program."

"Throw yourself wholeheartedly into teaching. A teacher must teach his students how to gather and utilise knowledge and wisdom from the randomness of life. One should be trained to teach. Oh and another thing, increase the pace of your PhD work. The topic is good. If you complete it soon, your chances of becoming permanent will improve."

And I berated myself for worrying unnecessarily when Rai sir was so invested in me. Nitin and Ashok often said that your supervisor takes your PhD very seriously, but doesn't care whether you get a permanent job. While having lunch with Rai sir, I realised they were needlessly pushing me to bring up the permanent job with him. After talking for a while, we walked to Birsamunda College's parking lot.

As we parted ways, Sir said, "Okay, Laxman, I will leave now. Do fill out the forms for a permanent position. No harm in trying." He got into his car, and I took off on my motorcycle in a different direction.

People like Veershwar Rai sir are indeed rare among supervisors and, I dare say, are becoming obsolete. I had just reached my room when

Rambadan called. Rambadan is a research scholar in the History department at Bundelkhand University. He failed to get admission at DU, so he returned and is now pursuing his research at Bundelkhand University while living at home. He was very fond of Rai sir, who was his favourite teacher. When I happily shared the story of my lunch with Rai sir, he exclaimed,

"Believe it or not, this is sheer luck. Higher education is no longer about subjects or ideas, it is about having the right connections and manipulation. They have defeated thoughts and ideas. There aren't any serious research supervisors left nor does research have significance in academics anymore. Universities are like grocery shops now, and a PhD degree is an expensive product of that shop."

"Okay, forget about all this. Tell me, what are you doing these days? You always talk so negative."

"I'm not being negative, I am afraid this is what is happening on campuses these days. Look at me, I've come to buy vegetables for my supervisor. After that, I have to tutor his son. This is the primary research process for my PhD. Sitting in Delhi, you have no idea about what is going on in other universities around the country. Delhi has neither the vision nor the heart to see the painful struggle of people like us, who are stuck in some remote corner of the county."

Sitting in my rented room in Delhi, I was listening to Rambadan's tirade, when I heard the loud roaring voice of the landlord, "The eleven-month agreement has ended this month. Your rent has been increased from three and a half thousand to five and a half thousand, plus electricity and water charges."

"But this is much more than a ten percent increase!"

"You may vacate the room, then. We'll give it to someone else. The property dealer is already offering to get me six thousand for it."

Saying this, the landlord left. A little later, I got a call from Amma. She asked, "All well?" I replied, "Yes." "Have you eaten yet?" she asked and I said, "I'm about to cook." After inquiring about my well-being, she hung up. I put the cooker on the stove. On the radio, after a volley of advertisements, I heard, "You are listening to Vividh Bharati's program, 'Aaj ke Fankaar."

It was the forte of his personality that he asked questions with full confidence, looking the other person in the eye.

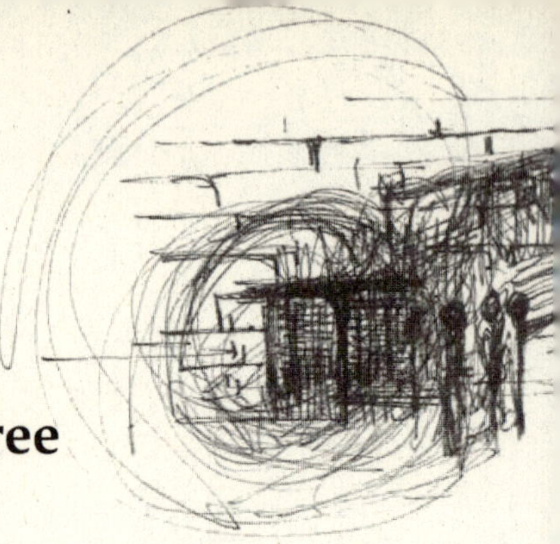

2nd January 2011

Two people and three Ad hoc Professors

Like the SIM card of a mobile phone, an ad hoc professor needs to be 'recharged' every four months. Yes, recharged! Otherwise, neither is of any use.

You must think, 'How ridiculous to compare a professor with a SIM card.' It is, unfortunately, the bitter truth. An ad hoc professor at DU is given a joining letter for only four months. Instead of getting a permanent placement, they are given a one-day leave and then 'recharged' again. This practice is common in most universities across the country - in some places, the period varies, in others the salaries or perks.

Today is the first working day of January, the day of contract renewal or the day of the 'recharge'. A clerk was sent from the principal's office to see how many people were present in the staff room. The clerk returned and said, "Sir, two people and three ad hocs are sitting there."

You might think of this as a joke, but sadly this is the reality. We have a different identity, and not in a good way. In the eyes of the system, we are just a number. Not human beings. Mere figures.

There is a lot of hustle and bustle in the college this morning. The letter hasn't yet been received and everyone is on edge. Some teachers-in-charge are looking down at the ad hoc professors with condescension as if to emphasise that their very existence depended on their mercy. Although everyone already knows which ad hoc professors will receive the letter this semester and which ones have been asked to leave. I do not know anything yet about the decision made in my college. Our joining process has been completed. After collecting the timetable for the next semester, I took the initial classes and, on my way back, went to the Campus library. I ran into two friends from Lohia College. During the conversation, they told me that Raghav from the Botany department hasn't been offered a joining letter this semester.

Raghav Bhardwaj has been an ad hoc professor in the Botany department of Ram Manohar Lohia College for the last two and a half years. In the previous semester, Raghav took practical classes with the 'seniormost' professor. One day he noticed a small error in the 'minutes' of the meeting, written by the 'seniormost', which he corrected. The senior professor took this very seriously, although Raghav was totally unaware. Meanwhile, the senior professor was waiting for Raghav's 'recharge' to expire. The day of contract renewal arrived. Raghav did not find his name in the ad hoc list, he went to his Teacher-in-Charge to seek an explanation. As soon as she saw Raghav, the TIC started venting her anger-

"Raghav, the students have many complaints against you. They have too many problems with you. That is why, I feel you're not a perfect choice for our department."

"Ma'am, this raises a question about your ability, because you selected me as an assistant professor. During selection, you saw my ability, but now you feel differently. How can that be, ma'am?"

Usually, Raghav does not speak up but he confronted her today. The other ad hoc professors in the department became scared. Raghav became the apple of everyone's eyes today because, even without correcting her mistakes, they had all been victims of that senior professor's wrath at some point or another.

Raghav did not know that as a professor, the basic principles he applied to his students, do not apply to the senior members of his faculty.

One is considered sensible only if one can adapt his values and behaviour according to the situation!

They narrated the entire incident with great zeal. I hadn't ever met Raghav, but here I was listening to this incident that occured with him.

In his academic training, the most fundamental principle Raghav had been taught was to ask questions. His professors at JNU loved him for his ability to ask questions. It was the forte of his personality that he asked questions with full confidence, looking the other person in the eye. He would never have thought that one day this strength would become his biggest weakness as a professor. Raghav was never seen again in the campus. Much later we learnt that he had become a professor in a big university abroad.

The profession about which I was feeling romantic and positive, seemed like a tragedy after 'four months'.

If you look around, you'll find hundreds of unsuccessful Thomas Alva Edisons in Delhi, awaiting their chance to shine while appearing for Interview after interview.

28th March 2011

Fears and Dreams

Today is my first interview for a permanent assistant professor position. There are two vacancies in the Hindi department at Samrat Ashok College, located on the south campus of DU. One post is for general candidates and the other is reserved for OBCs. As soon as we reached, Amarjeet, who accompanied me for the interview, introduced me to Manohar Choubey. He told me that Manohar understood the politics behind the appointments very well. He added that Manohar's ability can be gauged from the fact that he knew everything about everyone else, the past, present and future, just not his own. When Amarjeet asked what the scenario was, Manohar explained,

"As usual, along with the professors who have come for the permanent position interviews, suggestions of other names are floating around. Pramod Pandey is a sure-shot pick for the UR post, but there is a tug-of-war over the OBC seat. There are three candidates, but Ajit's chances are brighter because he couldn't get selected for Rani Durgavati College in 2011."

For me, listening to all this felt strange and uncomfortable. I have been very stressed for the past several days. The pressure of preparation for my first interview for a permanent post was unbearable. I prepared answers to all possible questions related to my subject. A few friends took mock interviews to help me prepare. All this preparation was just to overcome the tension that this was my first interview for a permanent post! I wanted the interview to go well. For the moment, it was immaterial whether I was selected or not. I was so stressed that something strange happened last night.

My interview began, but what was this? They asked strange questions, like 'What brought you to Delhi?' 'Why didn't you do your PhD from Allahabad University itself?' Another interview board member interrupted him and said, "There are no ad hoc positions available there?' How did you even think you would get a permanent position in such a prestigious college of DU?" Everyone started laughing loudly. The sound of their laughter could be heard outside. Their laughter was excruciating. I felt scared. Just as I was about to scream in frustration, I was startled and woke up. Oh! It was just a bad dream. I've been under too much stress. This was an old fear still haunting me. The night before each exam, I would have a demo test in my dreams, which always went badly. Sometimes my pen didn't work, sometimes I couldn't answer any questions. Big opportunities always intimidate people like me.

Many people, each more experienced than the other, have come for the interview. They have all come with impressive academic credentials.

Since it was my first interview, I had assumed that everyone would sit there and discuss which experts were on the panel and the questions they were likely to ask. After coming here, I noticed the interviewees were having a different conversation altogether. Everyone repeatedly mentioned the name of Professor Ramshankar Trivedi. Amarjeet, the so-called expert in the politics behind interviews and appointments began voicing his opinion, "Whoever is backed by Professor Ramshankar Trivedi will get selected here. Pramod Pandey's appointment here is certain. I've heard that Ramshankar Trivedi has given the nod. Pramod has been teaching as an ad hoc for 12 years."

Just then, a voice came from the other corner of the room,"'No, it is unlikely to be Pramod. His organisation, ABC, doesn't want him to get it."

With the confidence that he was revealing the real story, Amarjeet said:

"This time, he has ensured that the Principal sides with his organisation. Although the Principal is a Leftist, he gets along well with Ramshankar Trivedi these days. A person who hides his ideology to grab power chooses a misleading disguise. The lure of the chair can even lead to academic bloodshed. Every interview for a permanent assistant professor position is a shameless celebration of that bloodshed."

It made me feel like I was in a betting market or a marketplace, as I listened to all this. Here bets were being placed on professors. I started conversing with the person sitting next to me, who was twice my age. I was disturbed by what I had heard and wanted to feel at ease again. We introduced ourselves. The interview process had stopped meanwhile. It was lunchtime. Both of us went to the canteen to have tea. We were both more or less alike in this game being played in DU. Failing to pass off his age as experience, he asked:

"Bhaisahab, who is this Professor Ramshankar Trivedi? I've come from Ajmer, Rajasthan, for this interview. Till now I've written eight books and published eleven articles. And I've been teaching at a degree college in my hometown for nine years, on a meagre salary of seven thousand five hundred rupees. I came here with great hope, but after listening to all this, I realised things were already fixed. What will become of people like us?"

Tears welled up in his eyes. With trembling hands, he placed the teacup on the table and walked towards the Principal's office, bag on his shoulder. I couldn't fathom why he was telling me all that. Perhaps he empathised with my helplessness and felt he could share his pain.

After a while, my name was called. I reached the boardroom. Around a large table, five people were sitting like the five elders of the village panchayat. The person sitting in the Big Chair in the middle seemed special, the others were sitting on both sides. I didn't even come to know when my interview began and when it ended. I was asked a total of three questions,

"Tell us something about yourself. What was the topic of your PhD thesis? What is the relevance of Tulsidas' Ram Rajya?" On my way out, I couldn't help but wonder how they could have assessed my capabilities by asking just three questions in just two and a half minutes. The interview for the ad hoc post at Maulana Azad Delhi College had been much better than this. I returned with a bag full of degrees and a heart full of emptiness. The face and words of the gentleman from Rajasthan threw a dark shadow on my mind for a long time.

If you look around, you'll find hundreds of unsuccessful Thomas Alva Edisons in Delhi, awaiting their chance to shine while appearing for interview after interview. They are seen only at the time of the interview, then disappear only to resurface at the next interview. Their degrees force them to appear for each interview, even though they are aware of the futility of it all. Who is looking out for them in academic circles? Where do they spend the rest of their time? Who knows?

The academic world identifies itself with a few 'successful' people, higher officials, prosperous businessmen and their ilk, and pats its own back. Who is bothered about those who returned empty-handed from these campuses? It is these 'successful' people who gather at alumni meets on campuses and in hostels. They celebrate, form relationships based on their power and influence and go back. What of the countless other people who graduated from the same institution? Where are they when these 'alumni meets' take place? No one cares.

I came back to my room and thought It would be better to prepare for the UPSC exam. At least through the exam process, there was a possibility of succeeding based solely on my capability.

The whole system prepares the ground for compromises. Would we call this the opportunism of the individual who is forced to become a researcher, daily helper and family servant, or is it a feudal necessity of the system?

18th April 2011

The supervisor's comb

After class, I went to the Campus today. I needed some books for my PhD research. Just then, Vivek called and asked me to meet him. Although Vivek is one year senior to me, he's my junior in PhD. As soon as we met, he said:

"Laxman, come with me to the department."

"Why? What's wrong? You look very upset."

"What do I say? I never thought something like this would happen to me."

"Tell me, what's happened?"

"Ours is the first generation to reach the gates of these universities. Those people will never understand what a fellowship means to a backward Dalit researcher like me. With this fellowship, I can continue my education and save money to send to my younger brother who studies in Allahabad. But I'm very disturbed."

Vivek's words were upsetting. He looked broken. A while later, I asked him:

"You are under a lot of stress. Tell me everything, what has happened?"

"My supervisor has been harassing me a lot. He asked me to write three articles which he published under his name. I thought it was fine, he was my 'Guruji', and the thoughts were mine, even if it was his name on the publication, what was the big deal? But for the past four months, I haven't been able to apply for a fellowship. Each time, he comes up with some excuse or the other. Yesterday, he told me to look for two books and said I could get the application signed when I bring them. I searched for those books in the Central Library, Delhi Public Library, and even the Sahitya Akademi. When I finally found the books and brought them to him, he said, 'I have to go to the ministry urgently, come tomorrow and get your application signed.' When I went the next day, he hadn't come, he had taken a week's leave to go to Agra for a lecture. He is back today, and I want to give him a piece of my mind. Please come with me."

I become emotional when someone talks about the fellowship. We are people from a generation that began its education when it was still considered important and relevant. I grew up listening to my grandfather say, 'If you play and jump around you will fail in life, if you read and write, you'll become a nobleman.' Today the money and power of the bureaucracy have turned it into a modern form of the erstwhile 'nawabi' or gentry. Earlier, even an uneducated common man would sacrifice everything, including his land, fields, property and jewellery, to educate his child. Gradually, the connection between education and employment was broken and the very character of education changed from socialist to capitalist.

Today, Vivek said if he hadn't got a fellowship, he wouldn't have reached where he is now. Just one fellowship can change the fate of many, but those who consider higher education a hobby or pass-time will never understand this. This policy of awarding fellowships has brought about such a huge revolution in the lives of the marginalised families of farmers and workers, that research should be done to delve into this topic. From thousands of families, someone could reach a central university for the first time or even study abroad. One change in policy can bring about so much change in turn. That's why Mr Kanshi Ram called political power a 'guru-killi' or a master key. For people like us, higher education is a means to break free from the shackles of slavery. Mahatma Jyotiba Phule said:

'Without education, intellect is lost,

without intellect, progress is lost,

without progress, morality is lost,

and without morality, wealth is lost.

Without wealth, the lower castes are ruined,

A single ignorance has caused so many disasters.'

Lost in these thoughts, I reached the department with Vivek. Vivek was determined to confront his supervisor and say, "Sir, please sign my application today, I haven't paid rent for three months. I have borrowed thousands of rupees. How the hell can I write my PhD in these circumstances?". But as soon as he reached the department, the rebellious Vivek melted like butter. Instead of expressing his anger, he touched the feet of his supervisor, Dr. Abhinandan Kumar, and stood in front of him with folded hands. God knows how many Viveks have become 'professionals' in the politics surrounding higher education and academics. Today, his supervisor, Prof. Abhinandan Kumar suddenly thought of something and said:

"I am going to sign this today. But next time, come for the signature only after you have written the third chapter of your thesis. It is not right to take the government's money and do nothing. I had asked you to bring a proposal on the subject of 'Aadi Kal.' Why haven't you brought it?"

"Sir, The UP Higher Education exam is near, therefore I thought I would study for that. I've already written three articles. Please forgive me this time, Sir."

"Then, I'll sign on the fellowship only when you bring the written chapter."

"Okay, Sir, please suggest some books and guide me."

"Why? Why should I do that? Are you doing the PhD or am I? Work hard, run around. You don't do anything, just line up for the fellowship. This is not some charity, it is the taxpayer's money, understood?"

Professor Abhinandan Kumar was an Associate Professor at DU and my supervisor, Dr. Veereshwar Rai, was at Birsa Munda College. Abhinandan Kumar had come from JNU. Listening to the conversation, I thought that as far as erudition was concerned, there was no comparison between Abhinandan Kumar and Rai sir. As a research director, Rai sir's behaviour was completely different from Abhinandan Kumar's behaviour. Vivek was content that he was finally getting his fellowship after three months. While leaving, he said:

"Sir's wife is in JNU. She's going to be promoted to Associate Professor next month. Sir has asked me to write a proposal for her. Sometimes Guruji's behaviour is a bit rough, but he's a good person. He gets me to do his big and small chores. We are like family, you see. Once I made a mistake while doing something for him. He was supposed to go to the World Hindi Conference in Mauritius, therefore, straight to the airport from the department. He had just returned from Japan that day. He asked me to pack a bag for him. I brought everything he asked for - a towel, two sets of undergarments, a soap box, almond hair oil, and sunscreen from Kamla Nagar but forgot the comb. If you forget to put a footnote in an article, the guide will be upset, right? Tomorrow, I will go to his house and take some sweets for him, kaju katli and kalakand. Sir loves kaju katli, and Madam loves kalakand.It will make them happy. You know how powerful Sir is, don't you? He has connections high up within the Congress party."

Vivek went to the fellowship cell. On my way back, I thought how many researchers often go to the homes of their supervisors. Samir is familiar even with Dubey sir's dog. Sugandha goes to her ma'am's place in Vasundhara every weekend and rustles up new dishes for her. Everyone says that the most significant capability of a researcher is how close they are to their supervisor on a personal level. The admission process is not complete without that.

I remember asking Rai sir once, "Sir, if you wish, I can come to your house?" Rai sir scolded me, saying, "All the work related to your studies should be done in my college and in the library. I will give you as much time as you need. There's no need to come home. Instead of a scholar, you'll become a sycophant. I don't call any of my researchers to my house. Instead of thinking about coming to my home, spend time in the library." Seeing Vivek's situation today, I understood Rai sir's point that doing research, and not the household chores of the supervisor, will keep one's backbone straight.

When a young person from a village is forced by the system to compromise their conscience and become servile, a flatterer or a sycophant to survive, all too often their conscience gives in, for the sake of their dreams. That is why, when a young person chooses to become a sycophant of a supervisor, professor, or leader, it's not entirely their fault. The whole system prepares the ground for such compromises. Would we call this the opportunism of the individual who is forced to become a researcher, daily helper and family servant, or is it a feudal necessity of the system?

There are four types of ad hocs: cultured, tolerant, indifferent, and troublesome.

- Cultured ad hocs are ideal for this system.
- Tolerant ad hocs tolerate everything.
- Indifferent ad hocs are those who are doing the job due to some compulsion or to pass the time.
- Troublesome ad hocs. Usually, they are capable people who have been neglected.

12th February 2012

You can't get rid of Caste Identity

These days, the vice-chancellor Professor Markandey Singh is quite influential at Delhi University. His father too was a professor and vice-chancellor. Before he became the vice-chancellor, Professor Markandey Singh was considered to be a good professor. When the six and a half feet tall professor walked in the corridors of South Campus, students, who used to admire him a lot. would make a beeline to meet him. Today, he is the vice-chancellor of DU. As the new year begins, the entire campus is changing, both internally and in external appearance.

The North Campus is the centre of the University. It houses thc various offices and the vice-chancellor's residence. All the department heads also sit here. The South Campus is only an extension of the infrastructure of the North Campus. Therefore, North Campus is the hub of all kinds of activities. The Delhi University Teachers' Association (DUTA) office is also situated here. So, by default, being in DU usually means being in the North Campus.

This is the time when the semester pattern was introduced in DU. Together with the Knowledge Commission, the Sam Pitroda Committee had claimed to bring about radical changes in higher education, which were said to be linked to the World Trade Organisation (WTO). As a matter of fact, it was discovered that the government of the time had signed an agreement under pressure from global organisations, opening the door for private capital and foreign investment to enter the public education sector.

Students and teachers have united to oppose the semester system as they think annual examinations are better. A teacher engages in meaningful dialogue and discussion with students in the class. The students too get ample time to explore the curriculum and establish how it interacts with the real world outside. The semester system will turn this opportunity into an unnecessary haste. Teachers will be pressured to complete the entire syllabus in just a few months, and students will be pressured to take exams hurriedly. This will reduce higher education to a system that only awards degrees. Despite all the opposition, the UPA government at the centre implemented the semester system in higher education. Since then, undergraduate and postgraduate programs, across the country, have had exams every six months. Meanwhile, many state-level universities take five to six years to run three-year BA programs. This will only deepen the chasm.

In the past one and half years, the vice-chancellor Professor Markandey Singh has bestowed permanent positions on hundreds of professors at DU. Many people who had clout or held important positions were made permanent. Ramesh sir, one of the people who recently became permanent, said:

"This is the UPA government, where all kinds of people can get appointments. Professors were made permanent based on their connections. Everything happens in a planned manner, by number. My Guruji had already told me that I was number four. When three people got permanent appointments, my guruji rooted for me and I got one too, as I was next in line."

Ramesh Kumar Nirmohi studied at DU and knows everyone. Everyone knows him too. Today, he is expressing his happiness but is also worried about me. Ramesh's family, who were very cautious of the downside of flaunting their caste, added Kumar to his name after removing the surname associated with their caste. When Ramesh joined DU, he added a nom de plume 'Nirmohi'. I later realised that noms de plume can help in masking one's caste identity and avoid the trouble and discrimination one would otherwise have faced.

"That's what sets Sir apart from others. He's a man of his word. Once he says okay, consider your appointment in DU to be permanent. Once he has taken you under his wing, he will fight tooth and nail to get you a permanent job. He has never let anyone down, it is a record. What say, Laxman, come with me, let me introduce you to him. After that, you are on your own. Sir has a big heart, but you must make a place for yourself in it."

There were rumours that these days the university was running on the whims of Ravindra Rai, who was manipulating things from behind the scenes. Although he's the third or fourth-ranking administrator after the vice-chancellor, given his capability of 'influencing' he is practically running the University. Ramesh was very enthusiastic, but I could not go with him. Ramesh sir got upset and decided to take someone else, saying:

"You'll regret it. If you don't network and build relationships, you won't become a permanent faculty by sitting at home. There are thousands like you around. The pen and book will only take you so far; after that, you will progress only with the blessing of a 'high-up' with connections. Otherwise, you'll be left behind. No one will pay any attention. You'll remain an ad hoc faculty member forever. And one day, maybe you won't even have that, what will you do then?"

No one had ever taught me, nor told me so openly that in order to become a professor, one often has to leave behind their pen and books and even the qualifications earned with so much hard work. I used to think talented individuals easily get jobs in good universities without influence or connection. I used to think of myself as one of them, but after hearing this, I was completely disheartened. I was already hesitant to meet professors, call them, or seek their favour. Especially when I needed a favour.

Till now, I hadn't realised that this system of ad hoc and permanent faculty was so complex. Raghu da had shared his research experience with me long ago, explaining that ad hocs were of four kinds: cultured, tolerant, indifferent, and troublesome.

Cultured ad hocs are ideal for this system. They should be called perfect ad hocs. They can sense which way the wind is blowing. They know which path to choose to become an ad hoc. They do everything that is imperative for their calculative schedule. Initially, such ad hocs were scarce, but now they are found in large numbers.

Tolerant ad hocs tolerate everything. It is best to call them silent ad hocs. Once they get a job, they will do anything to keep it, no matter what the cost. Perhaps because they have no other option left or they are no longer capable of doing anything else. They are always ready to compromise and silently adapt to any situation. Therefore, calling them compromising ad hocs would be a fair assessment of their abilities.

Indifferent ad hocs are those who are doing the job due to some compulsion or to pass the time. They were unable to do anything else, therefore they became ad hocs. That's why they remain indifferent to everything. Such indifferent people are occupying a large number of positions.

Troublesome ad hocs. Usually, they are capable people who have been neglected. No one likes them. Their number is small. When they raise their voices and fight about an issue, it benefits everyone. They are the backbone of this system and are always targeted for it. They have a spine, which is why they have a voice. And because of these very reasons, they are troublesome for the system.

In this category analysis, there could be a margin of error, but every ad hoc does, more or less, fit into one of these categories. It can also be known as the caste system of ad hocism. Provided it's a karma-based system. Meaning, your actions and work show where you stand. No one can impose this system on you; you choose to be one of these categories.

The DTC bus took a longer-than-usual route and finally reached Mukherjee Nagar. I reached my flat with all this going on in my mind. These days, I have taken a one-and-a-half-room flat for rent in Gandhi Vihar. I have started cooking food myself. My beloved city of Allahabad came with me to Delhi in some of my habits. The staple of a student's life in Allahabad, the radio, is still with me. The radio is tuned to Vividh Bharti. And resonant voices of Yunus Khan from Vividh Bharti and of Ramdutt Tripathi, BBC London's Lucknow correspondent are fighting against the fear and doubt that has risen with Ramesh Nirmohi and Raghu da's conversations.

The higher education system awards medals only to winners. Those left behind are forgotten.

12th June 2012

Rakesh's Hanuman

These days, summer vacations are on in DU. After the exams, academic activities are paused for about two months. This leaves the ad hoc faculty in a lurch as there are no classes during the holidays . These long vacations are a happy time for the permanent faculty, but for the ad hoc employees, vacations bring uncertainty and fear. Before these vacations begin, every ad hoc employee is given a clearance and a termination letter. In this situation, only two things can happen after the vacations end: either the ad hoc employee will be able to rejoin in the new semester or he will have to appear for an interview. If the ad hoc employee's joining process is completed on the first day of the next session beginning in July, he will also get paid for the vacations.

If an interview is held after the vacation, it's as good as saying goodbye to the ad hoc job. If a department or college has already decided to get rid of a particular ad hoc employee, then it's certain, one way or the other, that an interview will be held. And if the job goes, then obviously there won't be any salary for the vacations. That's why these long vacations are not a time of relaxation and enjoyment for them but of stress and fear. Left to the ad hoc faculty, there would be no vacations at all. At least, they would get to keep checking every day whether they still have a job or not.

On the other hand, during these vacations, permanent faculty find time to finish their pending work. For example, they might go to a cold place to measure the temperature or explore the fundamental differences between the seas of Goa, Lakshadweep, or the Andaman and Nicobar Islands with their family. If both husband and wife are professors, they travel abroad. Meanwhile, an ad hoc faculty spends his entire vacation wondering whether he will be rehired on the first working day of July. Whether he will get the salary for the summer vacation. What he has today, whether it will still be there tomorrow.

Rakesh called today. It seems like yesterday when Rakesh came to take admission in PhD with me, in 2009. He had done his M.Phil from Hyderabad. He had studied at DU but couldn't get admission to PhD because his guide wasn't on the interview board and had asked the HOD to do the needful. The HOD admitted some other Rakesh instead. His guide made such a big fuss about it that, it is possible, no one named Rakesh Kumar ever got admission to PhD again. What was fate playing at?

Rakesh's guide was a strong-willed person. And Rakesh also took it to heart. He came straight to give the interview for a permanent position. He had made his guide promise him that the PhD admission fiasco would not be repeated this time. And that 'this' Rakesh would get a permanent job. Only after that assurance he booked the ticket and came for the interview. He hasn't yet submitted his M.Phil dissertation but he has become permanent. He has a lot of respect for me. He's throwing a party tonight.

Rakesh had a few drinks too many today. Since drinking was not allowed in my room, all the friends who were drinking went to the terrace to enjoy their drinks. I asked him, "How did you manage such a big feat?" Slightly drunk, Rakesh narrated the whole story, swearing me to secrecy.

"All this has happened due to the grace of my revered, worshipful, honourable, and esteemed Professor Ravindra Rai ji. Rai sir is a demi-God. He can mesmerise people. These days, he is solely responsible for the list of candidates who will get permanent jobs. Whatever I am today, it's all because of him."

Rakesh was getting emotional. I felt drunk without even having a drink. That night Rakesh just wanted to tell the whole story.

"You know, the wife of the younger brother-in-law of my Uncle's cousin is from the same village as our department head Professor Markandey Singh. And of course, being from the same caste had its advantages too. Markandey sir is from our community only, no? Markandey sir and Ravindra sir became my Ram and Hanuman and helped me reach my goal. Many people have become permanent thanks to these caste and community connections. Laxman bhai, you should also look for a professor from the Yadav community or someone from Azamgarh. Or else, find someone from Eastern UP and just play the Purabiya card. Books will only give you knowledge, they don't get you a job."

Rakesh is buying a new house and has invited me to see it in the evening. Just then, my landlord called and said, "Son, I need money urgently. Please pay this month's rent early."

That night, Rakesh told me something that blew my mind. He told me about a retired professor from BHU, Professor Bhagwandas Singh, whose three generations are professors. His two sons and two daughters-in-law are all professors in degree colleges. The grandson has recently been appointed an ad hoc faculty in some University with the promise of becoming permanent. If one counts both close and distant relatives too, there are almost 22 people who are professors. The service this family has rendered to the field of education is unmatched. We can find people like Bhagwandas Singh at universities and degree colleges in each part of the country. Rakesh mentioned DU saying that many small-scale Bhagwandas Singhs were found here too, who, along with their spouses, brothers, sisters, brothers-in-law, sisters-in-law and uncles, add up to dozens of professors. Provided, of course, they belong to the caste and community that has a God-given right to learning and teaching since thousands of years ago.

In this field of higher education, everyone has a different story. Some people manage to buy a house and a car in just three to four years after becoming permanent faculty. On the other hand, those who are the first generation to venture into the field of teaching and higher education, continue to live a student's life in rented houses even after securing a permanent position. I began thinking about my friends who had returned to their villages from Allahabad when I had come to Delhi. Those who used to sit on the same bench as me to study, God knows what their compulsions were, they left it all and returned home. I could never understand why and neither could the education system, which is like a marathon race with innumerable obstacle courses. Not all young people can participate in this race. A runner doesn't even look back after seeing his fellow runners stumble, fall and lose the race. The higher education system awards medals only to winners. Those left behind are forgotten.

In order to create a SOCIETY of slaves, you have to crush all possibility of resistance. It is necessary to compel SOCIETY to live in uncertainty and insecurity each minute to overcome resistance.

22nd July 2013

What is your full name?

In order to create a society of slaves, you have to crush all possibility of resistance. It is necessary to compel society to live in uncertainty and insecurity each minute to overcome resistance. Ad hocism is such a system, it creates uncertainty and insecurity. So far, it has been prevalent in the private sector, now it has spread to government departments. The number of resistance-less slaves is increasing here too.

Ad hoc employees must take a fair share of the blame. As soon as they get a four-month placement, they become caught up and begin thinking about how to get a four-month extension. They don't even try to link it to the system and its functionality and ask no questions. In fact, it doesn't even occur to them to wonder who or what is responsible for this situation. They find themselves unable to resist and end up blaming themselves. Those who believe in it, blame it on fate, while those who don't, blame the system. And that's it.

My mind would be in turmoil, asking why I should remain a part of the crowd. If it isn't a professor who tries to make people understand the situation, and inspires them to organise to bring about change, then who will? Once, I had a similar discussion with Raman Kumar sir. He began telling me stories about his JNU days, how he went from student to protester and even faced police batons while protesting against government policies. He would return and tell his professors about it. They would say if it isn't the academic people who fight for change, who would? What else could their responsibility be, in society? A person who compromises on principles loses his self-respect. As usual, he recited a relevant verse, from the vast repertoire that he had memorised, to support his point,

> zindgee tujhse har ik saans pe smjhauta karoon,
> shauq jeene ka hai mujhko magar itna bhee nahin.

All ad hoc teachers were made to rejoin the Hindi department of our college. There have been incidences in some departments, where I didn't even come to know when the ad hoc teachers were made to join and when they were let go. Only those who have been through it can understand how exploitative ad hocism is. Everyone keeps getting on with their lives. I mean, even we are no longer bothered that a young man of our age is struggling somewhere to make ends meet, washing dishes at a roadside stall, breaking stones beside some street, or working in a field with his spade and shovel. Everyone is trapped in a circle of their own making. We are trapped too.

✿ Compromise with you at each breath, Life?
I want to live, but surely not on these terms.

Brushing aside all opposition, the FYUP, Four-Year Undergraduate Program, was implemented at DU. A lot of drama happened around the implementation of this program. It was the dream project of the Vice-Chancellor of DU, Professor Markandey Singh, and after the opposition to its implementation began, he made it a matter of his prestige. It was circulated in academic circles that FYUP would bring up the quality of education to a global level, which, in turn, would increase the workload, creating opportunities for new ad hoc teachers. All student organisations, together with DUTA, the Delhi University Teachers' Association, were opposed to it. They believed that once the provisions of the Sam Pitroda Committee and the Knowledge Commission were implemented, the public character of higher education would change. Their biggest concern was that under the pressure of the World Trade Organization, public higher education in India would be opened to private and foreign investment. This would increase corporate profits but render education inaccessible to the poor, weak, and marginalised.

They dream of making higher education in India similar to that in Western countries. The biggest tragedy for higher education in India has been that most of our education ministers were uncaring and negligent. Those who did care were hell-bent on dissociating it from the country's social realities and trying to make India like America and Britain. The leaders who claimed to care did more damage to higher education than those who couldn't care less. They couldn't care less about the impact these policies would have on the marginalised and oppressed majority of Indian society.

A joint protest was held at Gate No. 4 against the educational policies of the then UPA government. Raghu da spoke at the protest. He said:

"India has signed an agreement with the WTO. The government is selling higher education into private hands. Now, corporate capital will be privately invested in higher education, and like new industries, new private universities will open. We will have to pay lakhs of rupees in fees for the same degrees that we were getting after paying a lesser amount or with scholarships in government universities. This process started with the new economic policies implemented after 1990. If not stopped, higher education will be forever out of reach of the marginalised and oppressed majority of the country."

The DUTA president, teachers, leaders, and student organisations held protests continuously against it. The leaders of the teacher's organisations thought this provision to be very problematic. From our college, Shakir bhai and I have started going together to participate in these agitations. My relationship with Shakir Bhai has deepened over the years. Although Mohammad Shakir is 15 years older than me, we started teaching in this college together.

The DUTA protest ended. We went to Pandit's canteen to eat sweet samosas. Suresh sent me a link on WhatsApp and said if I wanted to be permanent at DU, I would have to become like Sudarshan Shukla. We opened the link which led to a Facebook post. He had written a post for his senior, his ma'am, with twelve adjectives in the first line alone. Last time, Sudarshan posted a photo with his guru, they were together in a temple and he had written, "Here I am with both my Gods." Mohammad Shakir bhai said, "He who hasn't written even a line about his parents ever is now writing epics full of sycophancy." And I thought that Suresh was, in fact, a victim of the system, therefore he always forwards negative news. There were all kinds of people on the campus, not all were like Sudarshan.

In the evening, I met Shiv Naresh on the Campus. He was removed from his post at Makhimal College just because he had told his 'well-wishers' there to stop intimidating him in some manner or the other. He said that it was his life, he would live it as he wanted, that he would sit with and talk to whoever he wanted and who were they to tell him anything anyway. He had placed only one foot wrong. Today, Shiv Naresh is forced to look here and there after being removed from his ad hoc job. The reason proffered by the TIC was that the roster had changed and now the post was no longer for Scheduled castes, it was now for General category candidates.

In theory, UR or unreserved post means open to all categories, which means that any candidate who fulfills the eligibility criteria for UR can be appointed to a UR post. Simply said, candidates from any category, whether General, SC, ST or

OBC, can be appointed to UR posts. In universities, all appointments are based only on interviews. Therefore, only General category or higher caste candidates get appointed to UR posts. When interviews are separate for all categories, and no one else is called for the UR interview, only General category candidates will be selected, won't they? On the campus, this fraud has been going on for decades.

As far as higher education is concerned, a candidate's caste is often not very obvious. Once, Professor Ramadheesh Nayar told Ajit Pal, 'This is a General category post. You are an OBC. How could you come here for the interview?' But something terrific happened with Rakesh. This is how his interview went-

"Your name, please?"

"Rakesh"

"Full name."

"Rakesh Kumar"

"Father's name."

"Mahesh Kumar"

"Please tell us his full name too."

"Mahesh Kumar Pathik"

"Who are Pathiks? What category?"

"They are humans, sir. In that category. By the way, do you wish to know my caste?"

"No, no, nothing like that."

"Yes, sir! It is exactly like that. I understand what you mean. I have reached here only by fighting against people like you. In fact, I am from a Dalit family and am proud of it. God knows how I will work with people like you. You could have asked one question about my subject at the very least."

Saying this, Rakesh took his file and walked out on the interview board. Later, he became a PCS officer. But the Campus lost a genuine professor. Even today, someone must be sitting in that same place, asking the next candidate his full name.

There are four types of research scholars - ultimate, supreme, mellow, and fiery.

☆ Ultimate research scholars are individuals who, even before being admitted to a research program, aspire to become ad hoc professors.

☆ Supreme research scholars are quite like ultimate research scholars, but they get few opportunities to serve their Guru ji, mainly those which are beyond their capacity.

☆ Mellow research scholars tend to be more inclined towards studies and are primarily concerned about their careers.

☆ Firebrand research scholars, are those who are considered vociferous and outspoken.

28th July 2013

Four Kinds of Research Scholars

The existence and growth of universities revolve around research scholars. A research scholar is a crucial stage between a student and a teacher. An ad hoc faculty is the stage between a research scholar and finally, a professor. At times, one person can be both a research scholar and an ad hoc teacher, as the minimum eligibility for becoming an assistant professor in higher education in India is to get an MA degree and pass the NET exam. Therefore, a research scholar can simultaneously teach in a college. Many of my friends fall in this category. After observing closely, I have realised that there are four types of research scholars -ultimate, supreme, mellow, and fiery.

Ultimate research scholars are individuals who, even before being admitted to a research program, aspire to become ad hoc professors. As a result, research scholars in this category are most likely to become ad hoc teachers. They register or research under a supervisor who can unlock many doors to ad hoc positions. They become veritable shadows of their supervisors, following them from chamber to home, on social media and everywhere else they can. They are so devoted that before 'Guru Ji's' bag alights on his shoulder, they have already placed it on theirs. They firmly believe that carrying this burden will help them negotiate the crosscurrents of higher education. They are present even when they haven't been summoned. Their prime duty is to be present in the chamber before the supervisor's arrival and leave only after he has left. It is a part of their daily routine to accompany the supervisor to his car or the metro station. The supervisor too stays in good spirits.

Besides the above, these research scholars are also responsible for updating their supervisors about things trending on social media as well as the latest gossip and rumours circulating in the department. If a need arises, they are very vocal in supporting their supervisor and ensuring a favourable environment for him. To put it simply, ultimate research scholars have become the eyes and ears of the world of higher education. Earlier, their numbers used to be limited because there was less burden on supervisors, and also because they were more capable. However as the supervisors became incapable and overburdened, the number of ultimate research scholars increased. Nowadays, they are found in abundance and comprise almost fifteen to twenty per cent of the total research scholars. One ultimate research scholar can produce many more of his kind by being successful in his endeavours. That's why this species is growing at the fastest rate these days. They are the real scourge of higher education.

Supreme research scholars are quite like ultimate research scholars, but they get few opportunities to serve their Guru ji, mainly those which are either left over by the ultimate ones or are beyond their capacity. The difference between the two is only in the degree of sycophancy. Supreme research scholars fill the positions that require academic excellence. They fit into this system precisely because they are academically sound and can also be obsequious. Their numbers are also increasing in every university, comprising again around fifteen to twenty per cent.

Mellow research scholars tend to be more inclined towards studies and are primarily concerned about their careers. However, they lag behind the ultimate and supreme research scholars for two reasons - either they don't have the ability to be obsequious or they are unable to do so because of some personal reasons. They lack the flexibility needed to adjust. Most of them are the first generation to pursue higher education and come from deprived and oppressed communities. Neither have they inherited a legacy of obsequiousness nor is the environment in the universities helpful and supportive towards them. That's why they often vanish into obscurity after completing their research. Their disappearance doesn't leave any vacuum in the universities or the chambers of their supervisors. Because, in reality, they were never a part of the system. From university records to library books, their presence is documented nowhere. These research scholars have been the worst affected by this decaying system of higher education. Their numbers are estimated to be around fifty per cent.

Firebrand research scholars, as the name suggests, are those who are considered vociferous and outspoken. They are a rebellious bunch. Most of them are educated youth who have a deep awareness of their rights as a citizen and are vocal about them. They keep their eye on the changes happening around them and in the world. They raise their voices wherever needed, whether it's about attacking the system of higher education or the events happening in the country or the world. These young people are the ones who save higher education from becoming a dead, non-progressive thing. The system never accepts them, nor do they accept the system. They constitute only five to ten per cent of research scholars in any campus. The system doesn't want to include them as they have a voice and can stand up for themselves. That's why, as long as they are on campus, everyone has hope. Even if they are made to leave the campus, their voices continue to reverberate deep inside the university walls.

My fear has gone away...

5th August 2013

Reciting Faiz during the protest

Today, the teachers and students are again staging a joint protest against the government's policies. A crowd of students and teachers is blocking the road from the VC's residence to Gate No. 4. Those were the times when we first witnessed the powerful Trade Union DUTA fighting for a cause. A large number of teachers and students would participate in these protests. A protest is taking place today. Slogans are raised throughout the day. Around evening, the sky darkens and light rain begins to fall. People start dispersing. The then-president of DUTA, Nivedita Narayan, climbs onto a fallen barricade. Behind her is a large contingent of police, and before her, hundreds of protesters. She is holding a microphone that broadcasts with a breaking sound. The rain is coming down fast, and at that moment, amidst the sloganeering, in Nivedita Narayan's trembling voice, the surroundings reverberate this poem of Faiz Ahmad Faiz:

hum dekhenge,
lazim hai ki hum bhee dekhenge.

✩ We shall see,
Inevitably, we shall also see…

Witnessing this scene is one of the most wonderful experiences of my academic life. The past came flooding back. We were young people who had come from villages, from families of labourers and artisans and who inherited a fear of crowded places. We were instructed to mind our business and avoid dharnas and demonstrations. Time and time again, our elders and family members urged us to focus only on our studies and avoid politics and leadership. Maybe they knew the hidden dangers of participating in movements and demonstrations. My father was the only one who didn't advise me to avoid politics. I stayed away from movements and protests, keeping in mind all the advice.

My student life in Allahabad wasn't much different. My academic world stretched from the classrooms at the University to my rented accommodation. Those days, there was a buzz of activity during the student union elections. Right-wing student organisations were, not surprisingly, dominated by upper castes and also had the tacit support of some domineering teachers. The leftist and progressive student organisations could defeat them where ideology was concerned but they were no match for their muscle power and financial might. Despite these practical problems, socialist student organisations stood up successfully to the right-wingers. They included young men from labourer families in nearby districts. They had other challenges. They struggled to discipline themselves and be inclusive. The right-wing student organisations had a clear religio-cultural point of view and a large national-level cultural organisation backing them. On the other hand, whilst the socialist student organisations believed in the ideology of socialism, they lacked the training and the financial and manpower backing of a large cultural organisation.

These leftist student organisations would participate in this political wrestling match through study circles and posters and would lose. Nevertheless, they did not give up fighting.

Those were the early days of our BA course. We lived in small rented rooms, about 10x10 feet in size, which seemed like archaeological remains from Harappa and Mohenjo-Daro. There was only one way to enter those chambers, for humans and air. Only one person could live in that rented room at a time. Behaving like a sulking relative, sunlight never entered these chambers. The only beauty of that place was the books scattered around.

Pamphlets designed by a student leader were quite popular in those days. He would get many couplets printed with his name. I remember reading this on one of his pamphlets,

parinde bhee nahin rahate paraye aashiyaanon men,
hamaree umar gujaree hai kiraye ke makanon men.

Ten years later, I found out that the poem, which the student leader had published under his name, was written by Munis Barelvi, There's no other place quite like a university, where multiple generations exist together. Young people with means didn't live in rented rooms, they had flats. If the locality changed, the rent would increase significantly.

✧ To live in another's nest ne'er a bird went,
In rented homes our lives we have spent.

These rooms in areas like Chota Baghara or Daraganj were the cheapest, where flood waters came to stay and became roommates for three months. For the landlord, those rooms were a means of earning rent, but for us, they held a treasure trove of memories of wonderful days. Had he the means, every student wouldn't be averse to buying one of those rented rooms. Those young men who haven't done well, don't harbour such desires or wishes. No one pays any attention to them.

When I got admission in the MA program, I got a room in the Diamond Jubilee Hostel at Allahabad University. Before that, I used to live in Chandpur Salori. Each morning, I used to cycle to the university and my first stop was a street food stall, selling chana and moong dal sprouts, near Prayagraj Station. First, it used to cost two rupees per leaf plate, which later increased to five rupees. After that, I would rush to class.

We, the first generation of students from farmer-labourer families, spent the most beautiful days of our lives in the classrooms, the library, and with our wonderful professors and friends. Often, in some hostel or the other, we would witness political dialogues taking a violent turn with the use of crude bombs, sticks and batons. It felt scary to us and we would quietly distance ourselves. We were so intimidated by the violence and chaos unleashed on the crowds. This was when we were first exposed to politics. But we never participated in the protests and demonstrations for study circles, libraries and other important issues.

To be honest, the time of my undergraduate studies was that of selfishness. The sole reason for this was that having escaped from Azamgarh to pursue my studies, I had no desire to return under any circumstances. My elder uncle had already warned me, 'If you don't get good grades, just pack your bags and come back home quietly. Don't wait for us to call you.' I still remember how I had first come to Allahabad with a small bag containing two sets of clothes. In another bag, there was one kg arhar dal, two kgs wheat flour, one packet each of turmeric and salt, the spicy aroma from a cloth-covered bottle of pickle, some desi ghee, some sweet fried wheat snacks and an old twenty-rupee note that Amma had quietly slipped in without anyone else coming to know. I never had the guts to spend that note.

If Amma could have her way, she would have accompanied me to Allahabad, along with that bag. But, to tell you the truth, Amma did come along and was always with me, every minute, every second. Every day while kneading the dough, adding turmeric and salt to the vegetables, and adding the pickle to my meals, she was the fragrance of home that filled the entire room.

After I came to Allahabad, my brother and younger uncle also sent me a bicycle on the Roadways bus. I cycled from Allapur, Chand Salori and Chhota Baghada to Allahabad University innumerable times. Five years later, during my MA program days, I interviewed the famous writer, Neelabh, for the department wall magazine. After the interview, I came out to find that someone had stolen my old cycle. I couldn't even afford to buy another one during the MA program.

That strictly apolitical person from Allahabad has begun participating in protests and demonstrations. I still fear the crowd, but after participating in this massive protest by DUTA today, my fear has gone away. I have come to understand the important role of these protests. The clouds have darkened. Yes, the clouds cast a dark shadow on the campus. And the gentle rain has now quickened. I am unable to write what I was witnessing. Nivedita Narayan's voice is echoing in the sky, and people around her, drenched in the rain, are swaying and singing,

sab taaj uchhale jayenge
sab takhat giraye jayenge,
lazim hai ki hum bhee dekhenge

✪ Every crown will be flung.
Each throne brought down.
Inevitably, we shall also see… (Ttranslation by Mustansir Dalvi)

Our SOCIETY places books and pens higher than tools like AXES, TROWELS, HOES and SPADES. That's why even the ne'er do wells get respect if they are somehow associated with books, whereas the hardworking common man does not get the respect his labour deserves.

October 2013

Dozing off in class

An interesting incident happened in my class today. I was teaching the basic difference between medievalism and modernism. I explained how the world had chosen modernity, fought off medievalism and what impact it had on the modern period of Hindi literature. We discussed the social, cultural, political and economic changes that brought this transformation. This is a topic that deeply interests me. I teach this portion very earnestly in the history of literature class. I was writing a comparison between the two on the whiteboard.

"Two features of medievalism are evident, religious belief and faith. At the same time, the two basic features of modernism are logic and rationality."

Just then I happened to glance at the corner of the back bench. I noticed that Mohit had dozed off. I had pulled him up many times for it before. I approached him and gently placed a hand on his head. He sat up, startled, and then sheepish. I asked him to see me later. He spoke nervously when he came to meet me after class,

"Sorry sir, this won't happen again. I didn't deliberately fall asleep. Actually, I don't get much sleep at night."

"Any particular reason why you don't get to sleep?"

"Yes sir, my Papa remains unwell and my Ma works as a cleaner, sweeping and mopping people's houses. I am the eldest, therefore I have to provide for my education as well as that of my brother and sister. After college, I work as a pizza delivery boy, from 4 pm in the afternoon till midnight. Only after that do I get to sleep. And I have to be up at 4 am to deliver newspapers. That is why I don't get to sleep properly. And I really do wish to continue studying, that is why I come to college every day."

I began to remember stories of the struggles my Uncle, whom I called Bade Pitaji, went through for his education. Once, I had gone home from Allahabad during the summer vacation. That time, I had scored less in my BA second-year exam. After admonishing me for a while, Uncle told me his own story.

"I was studying in class 6 when the family assets were divided. The parcel of land we received yielded scarcely enough to fill our bellies. We took on a field for sharecropping, then ploughed and sowed it. Come dawn, I would harness the oxen to plough the field. By the time everyone else woke up, I would already be back. Then I would go to learn typing, and then to study. The tyres of my bicycle would be punctured in so many places that the guy who repaired it would get extremely irritated. I passed the senior secondary exam and wished to study further. I told Ma that the fee was sixty rupees. Ma had only twenty rupees. She borrowed twenty from someone. In the end, she could not manage to get the remaining twenty. I could not get admission in the BA course because we lacked Rs.20. I have seen days when there was nothing to eat at home except potatoes. For three days, a family of seven ate just boiled potatoes."

Generally, Uncle would scold me a lot more. It felt very natural when he scolded me. When he tried to lovingly make me understand something, I could comprehend that it was serious. God knows why he narrated this story that day. Later, I returned to Allahabad. But since that day, whenever I see only potatoes served for a meal, I begin to panic. Once, when I hadn't received my scholarship and the money sent from home had all been spent, one day, without realising, I boiled a potato. When I sat down to eat, it felt the potato had become the earth kept on a plate and that my whole family was ploughing it. That we were being sowed in it, like seeds. I could never eat potatoes after that. God alone knows why.

I put my hand on Mohit's shoulder and could only say, "When you are already continuing your studies while doing so much else, I will say just one thing…carry on. This hard work will never go down the drain. Success may come in any way but hard work and honesty never let you become a failure."

As he left, I could see a spark in Mohit's eyes. I watched him for a long time. In the subsequent classes, he never fell asleep. Or the days he did sleep, maybe he didn't come to class. But generally, he remained regular. Gradually, I could see an honest effort in Mohit's dozing off.

One day, five years later, he came to meet me on the North Campus. His mother was also with him. Showing her the Central Library, he said, "Amma, this is our place of worship, our temple, church, mosque and gurudwara. This is the place that has given us everything." His mother, an ordinary woman, was standing with her hands folded in front of the Central Library, as she would in front of a temple. Mohit met me and offered me a box of sweets, saying that if I had scolded him that day, he would have stopped coming to class, and that now he had got admission in PhD. Mohit's mother said, "Thankoo Porfessar sahib."

"Sahib'! Our society does not add 'Sahib' after every profession. Shoemaker sahib, tailor sahib, hairdresser sahib, washerman sahib, oil seller sahib, weaver sahib, sweeper sahib, shepherd ji, labourer sahib, farmer sir, you wouldn't have heard all these, would you? The epithet of 'sahib', this dignity, is it bestowed upon professions involving hard work? Our society places books and pens higher than tools like axes, trowels, hoes and spades. That's why even the ne'er do wells get respect if they are somehow associated with books, whereas the hardworking common man does not get the respect his labour deserves.

The funds received for empowering students from marginalised sections, half a century after Independence, were squandered on campus beautification and facades of buildings.

16th December 2013

The Vice-Chancellor's Pistol

Those who like and appreciate Professor Markandey Singh, the Vice Chancellor of Delhi University, believe that he worked hard to improve the university. One of his notable initiatives was "Antardhwani", an annual cultural festival that was kicked off with a lot of fanfare. The buildings, worth crores, lying unused after the Commonwealth Games, were now being used for DU's annual festival. The vibrant event is due to begin today. The teachers, staff and students from various colleges have gathered in the rugby stadium built during the Commonwealth Games. Looking at it all from an academic perspective, the entire complex has been beautifully decorated with the creativity of the students and the hard work of the staff on the directions given by the teachers. There are beautifully decorated colourful marquees everywhere and the stage was equipped with a powerful sound system. The entire university is there. Just then there was a flurry of activity.

The Vice-Chancellor of DU, Professor Markandey Singh was arriving at the main venue riding on an elephant. In the history of independent India, the vice-chancellor of a university never had the privilege of an elephant ride. An elephant is depicted in the logo of Delhi University since 1922. Seeing it walk around thus, the entire University went wild. And I think to myself, it is a small mercy that the logo has an elephant. What if it had a Buffalo? Would the VC have ridden a buffalo then? Actually, in our culture, buffaloes represent the common man and elephants represent the feudality and flamboyance of the royalty.

When we saw our Vice Chancellor sitting on the elephant, we all thought this swaying beast would make us permanent employees too one day. But later we discovered that the elephant had been hired only for that day. It took the mahout several days to get his dues cleared from the university.

All the ad hoc professors witnessed this grand spectacle with their colleagues. Those days, Professor Chiranjeev Kumar, a Hindi professor at Rashtrabandhu College, used to write satirical pamphlets for DUTA. This time he wrote that none of the later Vice-Chancellors had been able to follow the new tradition started by the then Vice-Chancellor. The vibrant event continued. A cricket match was also organised, in which some ad hoc employees were selected for both teams. Later, it was revealed that even though some ad hoc employees were chosen to play cricket in the Vice Chancellor's team, they didn't end up with permanent placements. The match ended in a draw, but the ad hoc employees who played in it are still playing the game of ad hocism without any result.

In fact, it was the same Vice Chancellor who had hemmed in the openness of the campus. The tea-mathri, Maggi and fried rice stalls in various corners of the campus were all removed. We used to sit there with our friends, seeking clarity on our research topics or locking horns over different takes on national and international issues. All those places where we used to get tea and snacks have been cleared. The Spicmacay building on the campus and even the bookshop near the law faculty haven't been spared. There isn't even a single bookstore left in DU now. Sharing an old memory Raghu da said one day-

"Markandey Singh is following in the footsteps of the previous Vice-Chancellor Desh Deepak. Earlier, this used to be a very open campus. We could walk from Mansarovar Hostel to Kamla Nagar through the campus. We would roam together, enjoying street food like the Rawalpindi chhola-bhaturas from Chache di Hatti, Brijmohan kaka's bhelpuri from his stall in front of Birsamunda College, and lemon and masala tea from D-School. Now it feels like being in a cage in a show."

Vice Chancellor Markandey Singh has made the entire DU as shiny as a newly minted coin, but now all activities that used to take place in the once lively campus have been relegated to classrooms. It came to light much later that the money misused for these activities had, in fact, been received in the name of OBC expansion. In 2006, a reservation of 27% for Other Backward Classes was implemented in higher education, with a provision that each university would receive additional funds, to the tune of a few crores, to build new classrooms and hostels, and for generally increasing facilities for everyone. However, most universities spent this money on renovating old buildings instead of utilising it for the intended purpose. The funds received for empowering students from marginalised sections, half a century after Independence, were squandered on campus beautification and facades of buildings.

In the context of Markandey Singh's elephant ride, Professor Tauqueer Anwar, from the history department of my college, shared a story from his student life. He said that the Vice Chancellor of Aligarh Muslim University used to carry a pistol. He said perhaps I wasn't aware that many retired army officers were appointed as Vice Chancellors or Proctors in various universities, just like retired soldiers are employed as guards. Did they think that they could control young students with pistols? The students who followed Sir Syed's tradition and wore sherwanis, literally made him run away. When he had gone home, the peon came searching for something.

The students asked, "What are you looking for?"

The peon replied, "Sir dropped his pistol somewhere when he ran."

Angrily, the students said, "Go tell your sir to get a cannon now."

An ad hoc faculty has no use for a tongue, he gets by with nodding and smiling.

14th March 2014

The Convocation and the Clerks

Upon entering a college or university staff room, it is easy to identify who is a permanent professor and who is an ad hoc. From whichever corner you hear the sound of laughter, smell food, hear discussions on recipes, opinions about buying clothes and even flats, conversations about who is going to make the next government and who is going to fall, a comparative analysis of new models of mobile phones and cars, they are all the permanent faculty. It isn't as if the ad hoc faculty are not allowed to sit with them. Old ad hoc faculty are present like the chutney at those gatherings. Upon looking closely, one finds that they have been reduced to a chutney, over time, in the grindstone of the system and they can be seen everywhere, adding zing to things. The old ad hoc professors are found in every corner of the staff rooms. But they always remain in the wings, never even fully participating in discussions, what to say of leading them. Even their body language has ad hoc written all over it - they sit with their tongues firmly tucked inside their mouths, their smiles are deliberate and artificial, their heads nod like pendulums, and their backs are forever ready to spring into action to serve their seniors. In short, an ad hoc faculty has no use for a tongue, he gets by with nodding and smiling. The new ad hoc faculty are generally found sitting disinterestedly in the outer circle in groups of twos and fours.

It is the convocation ceremony at Delhi University today. I'm going to receive my Ph.D. degree. I went to the college to take my classes. Jitendra sir asked me, "Laxman, aren't you going to the Convocation? You'll receive your Ph.D. degree." I replied, "No, sir. I would have gone but I am not going to wear the gown. I don't like it. I'll collect my degree later, from the office. When I had topped the MA program in Allahabad University, even then I had received my degree from the hands of the clerk. In DU too, I will take this most important degree of my life from the office only."

Jitendra sir said, "It is a big day for research scholars. People display their convocation photos, wearing gowns and caps, like medals. Although I didn't go to mine either, for I didn't want to be part of any remnant traditions of colonialism."

I said, "For me, receiving my academic degrees from the hands of the office clerk has been a form of resistance."

Jitendra sir and Raman Kumar sir often turned me in a direction that strengthened my self-respect but was detrimental to my career. I went to the academic office in the North Campus, received my PhD from the clerk, then returned to my flat.

The degree that I have in my hand today has a background behind it. This piece of paper reflected my journey. This was the first time in my district, my neck of the woods, that someone had received a PhD from one of the country's most prestigious universities. It was the biggest achievement of my academic life. There was a time when people would add 'B.A.' to their names after completing their degree – So and so Prasad, BA. After getting a PhD, you can add Doctor before your name, Doctor So and So. I called my mother to share the news that from today onwards, I'll be addressed as 'Doctor Laxman Yadav.'

And, in her happiness, she exclaimed, "I'll call you Doctor Sonu from now on!"

This evening, my elder uncle rejected my request, almost scolding me, saying, "A plate with Dr. Laxman Yadav written on it will surely hang on the main gate of our house. You may feel hesitant, but we want to show everyone so that they feel inspired by our efforts to educate our children. We want to show that we handed them a pen and a book and that it paid off big time. They will be encouraged to educate their sons and daughters."

Since the 1990s, all types of TRADE UNIONS in the country have been forcefully dismantled, whether they represented employees, labourers or workers. The railway trade union had the power to go on strike and pressure even the government to change its decisions.

August 2014

Trade Union shut down

The Vice-Chancellor of Delhi University, Markandey Singh, of the elephant ride fame, who thus managed to breathe new life into the logo of Delhi University, has issued a decree saying that DUTA (Delhi University Teachers' Association) is not a registered trade union body. And therefore, it should be shut down. This decision has angered all the teachers. When this happened, a few questions arose in my mind. What was DUTA? What does it do that a need has arisen to shut it down? What is its significance for an ad hoc teacher like me? And what is a trade union, anyway?

Thinking about all this, I reached college and had a long conversation with Jitendra sir and Raman Kumar sir from my department. They told me many stories about DUTA. On my way back, I went to the North Campus. Nivedita Ji, the President of DUTA, was addressing a protest rally there. I quietly joined the crowd, not wanting to be noticed. Although, ad hoc teachers are also participating in such protests these days.

Since the 1990s, all types of trade unions in the country have been forcefully dismantled, whether they represented employees, labourers or workers. The railway trade union had the power to go on strike and pressure even the government to change its decisions. Similarly, the trade unions of labourers and workers could march on Delhi from every corner of the country and force the government to change its policies. DUTA, the trade union of Delhi University teachers, has a similar history.

Except for DUTA, all other university teachers' organisations in the country have been made defunct or irrelevant. If they do exist anywhere, they submit to those in power. In this scenario, DUTA's voice is considered to be that of teachers of the entire country. There are two reasons for this: first, the number of teachers at DU is close to ten thousand, and second, there is a tradition of protest. It didn't matter whether the DUTA president was affiliated with the left or with Congress, each one of them fought for teachers' rights. The teachers rejected those presidents they found to be not so honest and open. Even when the right wing came to power, they continued this tradition. Raghuda had once recounted the history of DUTA, saying,

"It was 1997. A right-wing leader, Shri Anmol Rai was the president of DUTA. He gave in to the Vajpayee government on the issue of pensions. The teachers strongly opposed it.

After that, no right-wing leader became the president of DUTA for a long time. This is the tradition of this trade union."

Listening to Raghuda, I remembered my father who has a comrade, who used to tell me stories about trade unions across the country. One day, he talked angrily about George Fernandes-

"I think it was in May 1974. The biggest-ever railway strike took place under George Fernandes. At that time, George was the president of the All India Railway Federation, a trade union of railway workers. This movement changed the direction of Indian politics. It is said that Emergency was imposed in the country to deal with this resistance by the railway workers. George was a wonderful socialist leader, but eventually, he became a pawn in someone's hands!"

My father was a socialist activist and a comrade. He was involved in left-wing politics in a small district with limited resources, like Azamgarh. He would often take me to farmers' protests. He was the only one, in the village and around, who listened to BBC, London. He would sit us down, my mother, my siblings and me, and tell us about Karl Marx, Lenin, Bhagat Singh, Ambedkar, Lohia, and Kishan Patnaik. I recalled the stories he told us about trade unions.

I held onto my pen and book with more conviction. I started participating in resistance movements. I made resistance a part of my life. I recognised my strengths.

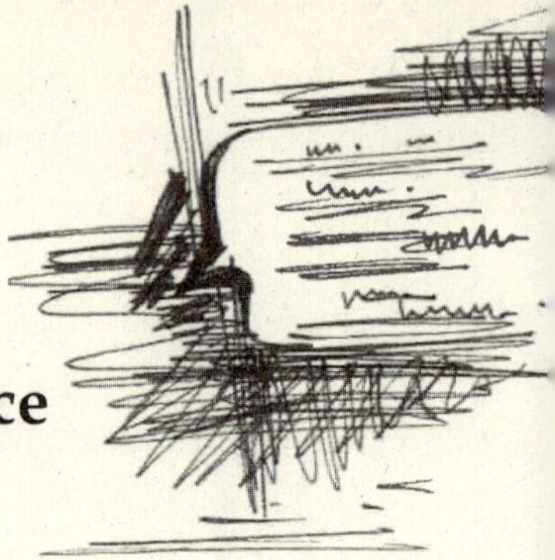

10th November 2014

Ranjan Kumar's advice

Today, when I reached the staffroom after teaching class, Ranjan Kumar, a senior teacher in my department, took me aside. Blowing smoke rings, he chatted to me, with friendliness and intimacy,

"So, Laxman Yadav, do you want to become permanent? Or not?"

"Why not, sir? I want too. Definitely!"

"But your attitude doesn't suggest you are serious about your career."

"I'm completely serious, sir. I am regular in taking classes. I prepare notes before I teach each class. I barely take any leave. I fulfill my responsibility towards the department and college. The students have good things to say about my teaching. I've published a few articles in journals listed by the UGC. I also have a book published this year. I've also filled out forms for permanent positions and given several interviews."

"Will all this make you permanent? What illusion are you living under?'

"Then what am I supposed to do, sir?"

"You socialise with those people; do you think they could help you get a permanent position? Yesterday, you were laughing loudly and glancing towards your right. Many seniors were sitting there, including a few of the principal's favourites. They took offence. Listen, Laxman! You've studied well, and you can teach well. Your articles have also been published. But how will all this get you a permanent position? If it were that easy, I wouldn't be telling you this. You're one of us; I care for you; therefore, I'm advising you. Stop hanging out with them. Why do you always sit in that corner of the staff room? Sit with the other ad hoc teachers near the kitchen. So many ad hoc teachers have come and gone. You, too, will go away unnoticed, just like them. Then what will you laugh so loudly about?"

Ranjan Kumar had almost finished his cigarette, and his counselling session was also coming to an end. I was unable to comprehend anything. I looked for that genuine concern in Ranjan Kumar's eyes, with which he would help get me a permanent position. In the evening, when I got a call from home, Amma could instantly make out the sadness in my voice. She asked, "All is well, no?" I told her that all was well, but today, in college, a senior professor voiced his concern that I was not serious about becoming a permanent faculty member. Amma reacted instantly, saying, "I too feel you are not serious about it. Do what they tell you to do."

By then, Papa took the phone and said quietly, "Never bow down to anyone, son. It is only a job; it isn't your life. Nothing is greater than your conscience and self-respect."

My father's socialist beliefs had become a source of courage for me. My elder uncle, a follower of the Kabirpanthi Satguru, would always say, "Whatever happens will be for the good. Just keep working honestly and hard."

What more does one need for a living conscience and true self-respect? Their convictions reminded me that I hadn't gotten this far by seeking favours, and they convinced me that I would never bow down in front of anyone in the future.

I had reached this far in my career without any help, solely due to my own efforts. And I would continue to do so.

This was the moment when I was, perhaps, most filled with fear and trepidation. But, at this same moment, I gave up my plans to appear for the UPSC exams. Forever. I also rejected Ranjan Kumar's suggestions for securing a permanent position. My fear gave me so much courage that I gave up all other career options.

I held onto my pen and book with more conviction. I started participating in resistance movements. I made resistance a part of my life. I recognised my strengths. I let reading, writing, and speaking define me. I decided to do whatever it would take to become a great professor, but I would never compromise my conscience or my right to speak.

Rohit Hum Sharminda hain.

Dronachari Jinda Hain!

Jai Jai Jai

Jai Bheem!

Jai Bheem!

Jai Bheem!

17th January 2016

Rohith Vemula's Sacrifice

It has been four months since Papa passed away. It was a cold winter morning in Delhi. Before leaving for college in the morning, I saw the news on my phone. It had been months since I had stopped buying Hindi newspapers. As soon as I saw one news headline, I was shocked. Rohith Vemula, a research scholar at Hyderabad University who wanted to become a scientist, had committed suicide.

Rohith Vemula had been on a continuous hunger strike along with his friends, demanding scholarships as well as justice against caste-based discrimination. The Hyderabad University administration was constantly ignoring their demands. Inspired by Baba Saheb Dr. Ambedkar's ideas, Rohith and his friends formed a student organisation known as the "Ambedkar Students Association" (ASA). During the last elections, the student association, which had the support of the ruling political party, was defeated by the ASA. After that, they became a target of the system's ire. Yet they did not give up their resistance. They continued their fight. To encourage resistance on an intellectual level, they used to run a study circle among their friends. They would introduce other students to the ideas of Phule, Shahu, and Ambedkar and join hands to struggle against injustice. They hadn't received their scholarship for months. Their hostel rooms were forcibly vacated. Rohit picked up a few sheets, for spreading on the floor, and a big picture of Dr. Ambedkar. He came out with his friend. For many days, he slept under the open sky. The university administration paid no heed. Thus, a research scholar who wanted to become a scientist, who fought against injustice, was ultimately forced to commit suicide.

No one had a clue that the news of Rohith's suicide would have such a huge impact on the country; that in the days to come, there would be a massive upheaval, not just on campuses all over the country, but also in society and political circles. Lakhs of people would take to the streets. A nationwide movement was about to begin. All campuses in the country hadn't yet been democratised. Thinking about all this, I reached college.

While I was teaching, a student asked, "Sir, a researcher at Hyderabad University has committed suicide. But why?"

"They were being wronged. They were fighting against it, but they didn't get justice."

"But it is wrong to commit suicide, isn't it, sir?"

"Yes, it is. But sometimes circumstances become so dire that... Anyway, you all must read Omprakash Valmiki's story 'Ghuspethiye'."

"Is the story related to education, sir?"

"Yes! When children from marginalised communities got admission to academic institutions for the first time, they were seen as intruders by those who dominated the system. How can a normal human being cope with such a situation? We need to create a better world and to do that having a democratised campus is a necessary first step.

On my way back after class, I went to the Campus. A few people were gathering at Gate number 4. The organisation 'Students for Social Justice' was holding a memorial meeting for Rohith. I stood there and listened to each one of them speak. A female research scholar was speaking in a choked voice,

"Many people like Rohith suffer caste-based harassment on campuses. Even the students who don't work hard get fellowships easily, while we face criticism despite working extremely hard. In our academic institutions, the SC/ST observer in the interview board, just sits there, munching cashew nuts. His sole concern is to please the principal or vice-chancellor to secure a place on the next interview board. He is least bothered about who is getting a job, and who is not. Who is concerned about what is happening in society? Those who have become permanent faculty are busy flattering the higher-ups for getting a job for their wives or their relatives. They are ready to do anything to help their kin."

"Whom did respected Kanshi Ram ask to, 'Pay back to society'? What these people are doing is just 'Pay back to self'. Otherwise, despite having so many Dalit and backward professors on the Campus, why is there no one to listen to our woes and help us? In such a situation, is it so unbelievable that a researcher is forced to commit suicide? They all, collectively, kill us a little each day, and then they call it suicide. What Rohith wrote in his last letter is not incorrect, that my birth itself was a mistake. We feel the same way when we come to these campuses - that being born a Dalit, an Adivasi, or in a backward household is a mistake."

"I am speaking boldly because I have decided not to bow down to these Dronacharyas (In the Mahabharata, he is said to have refused to teach Eklavya, the son of a hunter). These Dronacharyas will never be fair and just. My coursework was rejected because I objected to my professor's biased casteist comments and tried to correct him. He said I was wrong, but I know the truth. No one fails in coursework, but I did because he was paying me back for my 'insolence'. We suffer every day, but who will listen to us? If we speak out, our careers are ruined; if we don't, our self-respect is lost. This is the state of our campuses.

After Rohith's death, such movements should take place across the country, so that these dens of casteism are demolished. Only then will Rohith get a real tribute."

After the last speaker finished, the campus echoed these slogans:

Rohith, we are ashamed!
Dronacharyas are alive!

Jai Jai Jai Jai Bheem!

Jai Bheem! Jai Bheem!

PROFESSOR :

JNU is the top-ranking university of the country.

BREAKING NEWS :

JNU is a den of traitors!

Conspiracy to break India!

Traitors
living off
our tax!

8th February 2016

Anti-national Slogans and JNU

The new vice-chancellor of Delhi University has raised our hopes by mentioning in several public events that there will soon be many permanent faculty appointments. Forms have been filled out twice, once in 2010-11, when very few appointments were made and even those who had some political, administrative or insider influence were not absorbed. Then again in 2013-14, the vice-chancellor of the elephant-ride fame made some more appointments, but barely five hundred in all. Rakesh and Sunita keep asking me, "Laxman, do let us know when the form for permanent appointment in DU comes out. We haven't been able to secure any ad hoc or guest faculty appointments, perhaps we'll get a permanent position on the first try. There is a lot of corruption and nepotism in ad hoc and guest appointments. We have no godfather nor connections in any organisation or political party."

"Sunita, why do you think there cannot be any corruption in permanent appointments?"

"Because in ad hoc and guest appointments, the college staff collude and select the candidates they have already decided on. Everyone has his favourite candidate. In interviews for permanent faculty posts, experts are brought in from outside. Well-known scholars and experienced people are on the board. And that may lead to less corruption and more fair appointments. At least, that is what I think."

Is this the basic trust that a naive candidate places in the system or is it ignorance of the reality, I was unable to make up my mind. How many people would still have any trust left at all?

Watching Sunita leave after expressing her views, I couldn't help but think of the more than a dozen permanent placement interviews I had given till now. Sunita has come to DU after completing her PhD from a college in Haryana. I know her because her brother was my senior. These days, she teaches at the Open School and gives tuition, to cover her cost of living in Delhi.

By evening, JNU was all over the news channels. This university, which has been affected by the prejudices of the ruling party for a long time, has been embroiled in a new controversy today. News channels are reporting that some students have raised anti-national slogans in JNU. One channel showed a doctored video clip and even pronounced judgment on everyone.

That night, some of our friends at JNU told us that all the students gathered at Teflas. Student leaders said that the current right-wing government, unable to control JNU, was now trying to defame it so that no one could raise questions about the issues that have always been flagged here. JNU is the top-ranking university of the country. But the breaking news was filled with headlines like "JNU is a den of traitors", "Exposing the conspiracy to break India up", and "Traitors living off our tax money". Many TV programs and newspapers were spreading this propaganda. After that, a strategy was formed to destroy JNU. For the first time in independent India, a conspiracy was being hatched against the country's best university, and people were either silent or happy about it. What could be more nightmarish than that!

On the other hand, the Bahujan movement was gaining momentum across the country. It wasn't only the students, researchers, and professors from campuses all over the country participating in these protests, the movement had spread from cities to small towns and villages. There were heated debates in parliament, and a fierce argument between the HRD minister, the former chief minister of UP and a Rajya Sabha MP. However no concrete action was taken against the culprits in the Hyderabad University case. This was happening at a time when the campuses and streets of the country were witnessing widespread outrage and protests over the institutional murder of Rohith Vemula.

Teachers, hired by
a politician,
a contractor,
or the **education mafia;**
on a measly salary are making
this country
a Vishwaguru.

March 2016

'Tis Rama who pulls everyone's strings

I have come home after many years for Holi. Before I left for the fields, Umesh Bhaiya came home to meet me. He has a PhD in Sociology from Purvanchal University and has cleared the NET exam. He asked me about the ad hoc system at DU, and I told him that we get the salary of an assistant professor, but our job is only for four months. We are always afraid of being fired and our job is always in danger, for some reason or the other. He listened quietly. Then I asked him, "Where are you teaching these days?"

He replied, "I am teaching at Babu Khaderan Singh's Ramrati Devi Smarak Degree College in the neighbouring village."

I asked, "Are you an ad hoc or permanent teacher?"

He said, "I am neither ad hoc nor permanent. We are paid our teacher's wages daily. Everything at Babu Khaderan Singh's degree college is only on paper. There are supposed to be ten teachers, but in reality, there are only three of us. I was told they cannot give me the full salary of an assistant professor because they have to give a share of the earnings to everyone in the hierarchy above."

I asked, "What do you mean by 'share to the hierarchy above'?"

"It isn't like DU or JNU here. To open a degree college in this area is not an easy thing to do. Babu Khaderan Singh was elected MLA twice, but he lost this time. He has opened 3 degree colleges. He has spent around one crore rupees to build the infrastructure and get the necessary recognition. The students and teachers exist only on paper, in reality, there are none. Who will come to teach and who will study in the village? The students submit their papers and get their degrees, while the teachers submit their degrees and collect their salaries. This is the state of affairs in these degree colleges. Suresh and Har Govind have submitted their MA and NET degrees in five colleges, which means, on paper, they are teaching in five colleges. Altogether, they get twenty-five thousand rupees from all five colleges, but they teach only in one place. And that cannot be called teaching! They just go to mark their attendance."

I asked, "I don't understand, bhaiya. How can someone collect salaries from multiple places by simply submitting their degree?"

"This is what happens here. Look at Azamgarh, for example. There were six government degree colleges here earlier, and around 10,000 students enrolled each year. Today, the number of degree holders has doubled in this area, but the government has reduced the funding for these colleges. No new teachers have been recruited. The largest degree college in the district has 12 departments. Nine of them do not have a single permanent professor today. Can you understand why it is so? It's because the politicians and contractors are laundering their black money to white through these private degree colleges."

I asked, "How do private degree colleges launder black money?"

He replied, "See, when a degree college is opened, they show one building and get approval for three courses. For example, they show a teacher's salary to be fifty thousand rupees on paper but keep twenty-five thousand for themselves. They give twenty thousand as a bribe to everyone else from the university to the politicians, and pay five thousand to the teacher. The remaining amount is used for other businesses or the next election. This is considered a safe investment option. That's why we have no choice except to work for five thousand rupees. Only now have I realised that to become a professor was a wrong decision. I can't leave my family behind and go to Delhi or Lucknow. I have to live my life like this, there is no option. Come, let's go, we have to water the wheatfields."

I am an ad hoc professor, based in Delhi, and I used to think I was the biggest victim of injustice. But after listening to this story, I realised that the real game of higher education is being played in these small towns and villages. So many talented young people are mortgaging their futures to write the destiny of this country. Teachers, hired by a politician, a contractor, or the education mafia; gurus on a measly salary are making this country a "Vishwaguru" (A guru to the world). This is the reality of today's "Vishwaguru".

The real qualifications were UNWRITTEN. And how could we read something that hadn't been written?

This unwritten thing is known as JUGAAD.

26th April 2016

Abhijyan's Wedding

Gradually, it dawned on us that degrees were only a written qualification necessary to become a professor. The real qualifications were unwritten. And how could we read something that hadn't been written? This unwritten thing is known as 'jugaad'; influence, clout, knowing the right people. While we accumulated written qualifications, those who also learned to apply 'jugaad' are the bosses today. Anyway, we have to make a place for ourselves in these circumstances. Every temporary employee feels exhausted trying to make a place for himself in this academic world.

The fight of the ad hoc professor is to be recognised as a 'guru' or teacher in a country that claims to be a 'Vishwaguru' (world guru). The capable ad hoc professors create their world within a limited circle of concern and colour it according to their capacity. A temporary teacher or employee thinks about planning a family but cannot make any decision due to the uncertainty. An unemployed person cannot gather the courage to get married while still waiting for an ad hoc job. Sanjana's family found a match for her and the groom's family did not want a daughter-in-law who works. Therefore, Sanjana's family got her ad hoc job terminated and married her off. She could no longer pursue her dream and was forced to embark on a different journey.

Abhijyan Prakash has been teaching at Swami Sahajanand College for many years. Today, it is his wedding day. His family members, relatives, friends and the bride are all waiting for him in Faizabad. But today is his last working day. If he hadn't signed the attendance register today, Abhijyan would have lost his job. He had no choice.

Abhignaan went to the college, signed the attendance register, and took today's class. Then he directly took a flight to Lucknow. When I spoke to Abhijyan, he was going to Faizabad from Lucknow. It was already 6 pm. Later, Abhignaan told me that he reached his home at 8 pm. Finally, he could dress up in his groom's finery.

That night Abhignaan said, "If I had a permanent job, this wouldn't have happened." He hid his frustration, saying,

"We get married only once. I had dreamed about this day. But I had never thought it would go the way it did. Remember my advice, get married when you get a permanent position. Or else during the holidays."

The Yashpal committee had advocated that higher education be FREED FROM BUREAUCRATIC SHACKLES and that scientific thinking be encouraged among professors. However, these days, TEACHERS ARE FORCED TO BE LIKE OFFICE CLERKS.

4th May 2016

Bhagat Singh Was Not Ad hoc

Today, the UGC issued a notification regarding the Third Amendment. It aims to increase the daily teaching hours and introduce new practices in higher education. This means that the workload will be reduced by half. The impact of this reduction will be felt across the country. The amendment also states that all colleges will have biometric attendance and every teacher must spend at least five hours on campus.

I began reading the recommendations of the Professor Yashpal Committee on the internet today. The committee had advocated that higher education be freed from bureaucratic shackles and that scientific thinking be encouraged among professors. However, these days, teachers are forced to be like office clerks. Everyone hopes that DUTA will lead the fight against this. Delhi University Teachers' Association has rolled up its sleeves

DUTA has formed separate teams to mobilise teachers in all colleges. Imagine! Professors need to be convinced and motivated to fight for their rights. Several senior activist teachers from DUTA have come to my college and are in the process of mobilising the teachers. A few pick up their registers and go to their classrooms, while others leave to drink tea. Ad hoc teachers are the first to get away, lest someone see them there.

In our college, ad hoc teachers participate equally with permanent professors in these meetings. Even in department meetings, and the 'Staff Council', the largest meeting in the college, ad hoc teachers sit beside the permanent faculty. But, an ad hoc professor doesn't get a chance to speak in any of them. No one finds it the least strange. It's as if the ad hoc teachers are considered their equals just by sitting together in the meetings. Ad hoc professors have also decided not to speak up in a meeting, no matter how important the issue is. However, there are exceptions everywhere.

In Maharaja Suheldev College, I had a good relationship with an associate professor from the history department, Rupendra Chaudhary sir. I met many like-minded individuals with whom I could always discuss people's movements. Such people have played a significant role in making me fearless and daring. Rupendra sir was well-known for his straightforwardness and commitment. He was also known for raising democratic slogans during protests. I often discussed government policies with him. When I met him today, he said-

"Laxman! Don't you get it? they just want to turn higher education into a grocery store. I am sure you remember Sam Pitroda and the Knowledge Commission. Now they're doing the same thing again. They are trying to turn higher education into a profit-making enterprise in an open market, on a global level. The Congress implemented it gradually, but the BJP government has hastened the process considerably. They have signed an agreement with the World Bank to allow foreign investment in higher education. All this is happening to make education a business. In this way, capitalists can make a profit from education too."

Dr. Abhayanand Tripathi, an ad hoc teacher sitting with us, said, "Look, Rupendra sir! We don't know much about politics and we won't be able to do anything about this by ourselves. If we're thrown out, everyone will be thrown out. And if we're saved, everyone will be saved. By ourselves, we won't be able to do anything, nor stop anything from happening."

"Dr. Abhayanand, if all professors start thinking like you, nothing will be left to save. If Bhagat Singh, Sukhdev, and Rajguru had thought like this, would we have gained Independence?"

"Rupendra sir, you are a leader of the DUTA. With people like you in DUTA, we will surely be saved. Bhagat Singh wasn't an ad hoc teacher. He didn't have to pay EMIs. He didn't have a wife or children either."

"Don't forget, we are living this life today because of people like them. In the future, if there is no one left in DUTA who can fight, then whatever government orders come, we'll just have to follow them. Take this Third Amendment, for example. Thousands of teachers have suddenly lost their jobs."

"Yes, sir, if all ad hoc teachers come to save their jobs, I will also think about it. I will take your leave now, I have to take my son to the stadium. His swimming classes are on these days."

A temporary employee can neither have an opinion nor affiliate with any organisation. They are loyal only to the ruling political party.

31st May 2016

I Hate Politics

There's a DUTA rally from Mandi House to Sansad Marg today. My college is near Mandi House. Whenever DUTA organises a big rally, all classes are suspended. Lately, the number of teachers from our college participating in the protest has increased. Today, when all ad hoc teachers have lost their jobs, everyone expected this number to be greater. When we asked Professor Raghunandan Vajpayee, an ad hoc teacher, to join us, he said, "Even during India's freedom struggle, not everyone was out protesting on the streets. If there are five thousand of us, we'll either save everyone or lose everything together. Today, I am supporting DUTA in absentia."

As we left for the rally, we saw how many ad hoc teachers were still taking classes despite the suspension. Just then the bell rang, and they came out. We asked, "Won't you join the DUTA protest? Now that we've lost our jobs." One of them retorted, "I'm a teacher. My first duty is to take classes. Whatever fate wills, will happen. You go, I don't want to. I hate politics."

The young generation of our times is being weaned on this phrase 'I hate politics!' it is ironic that politics itself is doing this. Our colleague Dr. Tauqeer Anwar said,

"Let him go, he is a 'sanskaari', a tradition-bound ad hoc teacher. He won't join the protest. His boss is close to the PVC. One can say they have the ear of the VC himself. He has secured a permanent job and cares only about himself. Like a horse wearing blinkers can only see the ground beneath its feet, humans nowadays see only to their interests."

On our way to the rally, we met some more ad hoc teachers who were frustrated too. Even a single frustrated ad hoc teacher is enough but if a few of them join hands, they can make a big impact, joining the DUTA protest I realised that the government's decision had turned many 'sanskaari' and tolerant ad hoc teachers into rebels. Ranjan, who previously had been quiet and laid-back, was now boldly expressing his anger, saying,

"Our lives have been ruined. Before 2014, what didn't I do as a Congress supporter? No one from the Congress made me permanent. I've been carrying the Sangh's mantle for the past two years. And now this BJP government has taken my job away. When I used to say our government is in power now, and permanent appointments should be made, they would say the VC is not ours yet, the principal is not ours yet... If we bring it up in Sangh, they tell us to be patient, everyone will get a permanent placement in time. When I was supporting the

Congress, I was scorned for the semester system and FYUP, now with the BJP my job itself is gone. Listen to the slogans being shouted over there,

'Gobbled up our jobs, turned down the thumb, there isn't any doubt, good days have come!"

Today it is crystal clear to me that a temporary employee can neither have an opinion nor affiliate with any organisation. They are loyal only to the ruling political party. It's a lesson in adapting to the situation and applies to most professors and government employees. Today's rally was an attempt to challenge this situation. As we left the rally, Raman sir recited a verse:

> log kalmon se banate hain kagzon par kuyen,
> aur ummeed ye karate hain ki panee nikle.

✿ With pens, they draw wells on paper
And expect earnestly to draw water.

Baba Saheb fought for us in that time and age. If we are unable to fight today, it's a shame.

July 2016

Listening to Ramjanam's story from Raju

Ramjanam da is our senior. Before, as a researcher, he was known for his leading questions and debates. We met on the Campus. While having tea, he said,

"You know, Laxman bhai, I used to work as a labourer in Delhi. I used to work at night and distribute newspapers in the morning. My father is a mason. I too have done manual labour in my childhood. I wanted to study, therefore I ran away from home one night and caught a train to Delhi. I got enrolled in Shahuji Maharaj College. I cleared JRF on my first attempt and funded the education of two siblings with the fellowship. Now, the fellowship is over, and my father is ill. I have given interviews at many places. What to talk of an ad hoc post, I don't even have a guest lecturer position. Have I made a mistake in leaving the mason's tools and taking up a pen? Will I need to work as a mason once again?"

Ramjanam da comes from a very deprived family in Purvanchal, Uttar Pradesh. The same place Rakesh sir had once mentioned, saying there was a need to connect with the people. I shared this with Ramjanam da:

"Sir, you should meet Professor Ravindra Rai once. I've heard he's helping people from Purvanchal get permanent placements. You're also from Purvanchal."

"You're still a child, Laxman! Regionalism comes only after casteism. Just as people living in one region may not be the same, my being from Purvanchal doesn't necessarily mean someone considers me close. I was never good at flattering people. I have worked hard to reach here. I don't wish to go back to my village. For us, villages are deep dark wells of casteism and feudalism. Cities have accepted us with open arms and made us feel normal. Even if I cannot be one, I will ensure my children become professors one day."

We have seen Ramjanam da often on the research floor, always wearing clean pants and a bush shirt and carrying a rucksack. He also used to bring a water bottle and some soaked black gram. One day, when he offered us some black gram, we asked him, "Sir, why do you bring chana in the water bottle?" He replied, "I soak the dry chana in water and keep it in the bottle. By afternoon, they are ready to eat. Eating out every day is not good for health." He would eat the thirty rupees meal with us at Joshi's dhaba, to his full. Then, he would return to the research floor. He was the first to go to the central library, and the last to return. I suggested going for tea in his room one day, but he refused. Ajay was closer to him. He insisted and we went with Ranjanam da to his room.

It was a tiny chicken coop of a room in the Christian Colony, near the Campus. A damp and musty room next to the common toilets. Feeling somewhat ashamed Ramjanam da said, "Now, how do I invite someone to my room? I only come here to sleep and bathe. The rest of the time is spent on the Campus. I am not even getting a guest lecturer position anywhere. How long will I manage my expenses by proofreading?"

Ramjanam Da has a very nice picture of Baba Saheb in his room. Apart from that, there is a neat bed and many books. I was reminded of my childhood friend Raju from my village. He was my dearest friend and lived in the 'Chamrouti', a Dalit colony, southwest of the village. He was an excellent player on our inter-village cricket team and was very talented. His writing was as beautiful as a craftsman's work. He loved books. He kept a picture of Dr. Ambedkar and a few books in his decrepit hut. We had won many matches together for our village team. Like me, Raju was also afraid of conflicts. He often said, "Sonu Bhau, we will do something big in life."

He was deeply inspired by Baba Saheb, Dr. Bhimrao Ambedkar. He used to learn to read and fight from him. He gained the courage to dream big from these books and ideas. He contested the student union election in the degree college but lost. He said, "At least I stood for the election, so what if I lost?" He was very courageous. Often, he said, "Baba Saheb fought for us in that time and age. If we are unable to fight today, it's a shame." He would often get upset and angry when he saw the arrogant behaviour of the so-called upper castes in the village and heard their abusive comments. The ne'er do well boys of the village would get drunk and often create a ruckus in Chamarouti. He would get furious. He would avoid our gaze the next day, and ask us, "Why do they do this to us?" His eyes would ask many difficult questions, for which we had no answer. Raju's mother was the village midwife. We were born in her hands. We owed our lives to her.

My socialist father's open-mindedness had opened the doors of the 'Chamarouti' for us, which otherwise opened only for labourers or to distribute leftover food. Respected Kanshi Ram's mission had instilled self-confidence in the Dalit settlements of UP, but it reached our village late. Raju was the one who brought it. I had been away from the village for ten years and returned after my father's untimely death. The villagers welcomed me with affection. Raju stood quietly in the distance. When the others began to leave, he came near and kept his hand on my shoulder. His eyes also filled with tears. He couldn't speak. If we had been playing cricket, he would have hugged me tightly.

Rohith, We can't even bid you farewell. You haven't gone anywhere. You have become the strength of our struggles. You have become the hero of every fight for social justice on campuses, all over the country. You are our courage. You are alive within us.

JaiBheemComradeRohith!

17th January 2017

A Murder in DU

It is a grim day. A professor had been teaching in the music department of a Delhi University college for almost seven years on an ad hoc basis. He had been harassed for months. He passed away due to a cardiac arrest. A condolence meeting was held for him, in front of the Vivekananda statue on the Campus. Janardan Mishra, the former president of DUTA, spoke with great anguish,

"The professor has not died a normal death. It's a murder. Our entire system has become a murderer. Do our young friends leave other careers and become professors only to face this? Will talented young people still dream of becoming professors after such incidents? Can we save our universities in these circumstances?"

Everyone bid a tearful farewell to the ad hoc professor. People talked about how the principal and TIC of his college had been harassing him for a long time. He could make out that he wouldn't be made permanent. He used to remain sad. The depression and the increasing pressure ultimately took his life suddenly last evening.

His heart couldn't take it any more.

After the condolence meeting, I went to the Central Library. I tried to do some reading, but my mind was very restless. We organised a protest meeting today on Rohith Vemula's martyrdom day. Who knew I would have to attend another condolence meeting too? Many friends are calling and messaging people for the evening's protest meeting, but I'm sitting on the research floor, filled with restlessness. I am supposed to give a speech this evening. Sitting here, I tell myself that I should prepare for it. I started writing a letter to Rohith Vemula.

Dear friend Rohith, today it's been a year since you were 'murdered by the institution.' Innumerable young people like me read your last letter and feel anger and grief. It also helps us make new resolutions and decisions. Your dreams are still alive in many eyes. Numerous voices still echo the slogans you raised. You are still very much present, I wish you could see that yourself.

You didn't have to give up, friend. You had to fight, even though it wasn't at all easy. Although, you did sharpen this struggle of thousands of years to a point. The whole society was shaken. Such moments are rare. I wish you could have seen the strength you've evoked even in distant villages. The academic fortress you challenged is starting to crumble today. I wish you could have seen that your pictures are not only on walls but in people's hearts too. You won the battle of ideas. You have awakened the sleeping, deprived and backward, Bahujan youth both within and outside the university.

Dear friend Rohith, you know that the atmosphere on campuses is changing, all over the country. While on the one hand, awareness has increased among the marginalised and deprived youth and they are speaking out, those in power are becoming more subtle in their attacks. The government that stopped your fellowship for months is stopping everyone's fellowship now. Seats have been reduced by half. You have become the face of resistance that seeks answers to the basic questions of higher education.

You know, Rohith, a lot has changed. If you were here, you would be happy to see that Ambedkar is the hero of every struggle that is taking place on the streets of India today. Rohith, we never had a chance to meet, but in all these days, the person I have met every day is you. Because what I saw in you, I haven't seen anywhere else. There was an honesty about you, both ideologically and intellectually. Had you been alive, I would have invited you to DU many times by now. We have raised slogans in your name, you are still alive in our unfulfilled dreams. You are alive in our struggles. You are alive in every clenched fist. You know, we have organised a programme in your name, today. Had you been here, you would have given a speech. You would have spoken in a broken Hindi. Our hearts, broken in these shared struggles, would have found solace.

We can't even bid you farewell. You haven't gone anywhere. You have become the strength of our struggles. You have become the hero of every fight for social justice on campuses, all over the country. You are our courage. You are alive within us.

Jai Bheem friend Rohith!

If you are an ad hoc professor belonging to a marginalised section of society, the system exploits you in many ways at the same time.

February 2017

Career and Motherhood

While returning from college, I met Aparna on the North Campus today. Aparna had been a co-researcher during my PhD coursework. She is currently an ad hoc professor at Rani Durgavati College. Whenever we met on the Campus, she would laugh and share stories about her college. She was the one who had told me that in a women's college, one finds all kinds of mother-in-law figures because of the way the senior professors behaved with the juniors. She would mimic Khatri Ma'am and Sahni Ma'am perfectly. Her favourite story was about clothes. For example -

"Listen, Aparna, I'm your senior, how dare you ignore my brand-new dress?" Aparna's mimicry was so good that we would laugh till we cried. Then she would quietly remind us not to tell anyone, or she would be in trouble.

But today, Aparna looked very upset. I asked her:

"What's wrong? You seem very disturbed."

"Yes, I am. A lot."

"Tell me, what happened? Is everything fine in college?"

"What could be wrong with the college? It was fine before I taught there and will remain fine after me. But I still don't know whether I am fine or not."

"But what happened? Tell me."

"I made a big mistake. I wanted to have a baby. You know I've been an ad hoc professor for the past seven years. In seven years, I've been thrown out of three different colleges. The first time, I was thrown out after only one semester because the new TIC wanted to appoint their researcher as an ad hoc professor. Then, I taught for one semester at another college, thirty-five kilometres from my house. The same year, I got married. I had to resign from that college due to the circumstances. After that, I didn't get a job for a whole year. Then, I got a job at Rani Durgavati College in July 2012. I've been teaching there for four years. My family kept saying it's been so many days since I married and I shouldn't wait to become permanent. It was high time I had a child. I kept delaying it because I didn't want to compromise on my career. But then I thought there was no imminent chance of becoming permanent, and I planned to have a baby. Now I feel as if I've made a mistake. Today, I learned that ad hoc professors don't get maternity leave."

Her eyes were filled with tears, and I could see her helplessness and anger. The young woman who always laughed and joked about looked sad and upset today. I was stunned. I tried to console her,

"Don't worry, Aparna, all will be well."

Apart from these generic words, I had nothing else to say.

"Nothing will be fine, Laxman. We almost lost our jobs in June. I was so worried then. I had fought with my family for the first time, to go for the DUTA protest. Somehow, we managed to hold on to our jobs at that time. And now this is happening. Did I commit a crime by planning a baby? Am I not human?"

I looked at her tear-filled eyes and then looked away, feeling utterly helpless. I too am an ad hoc professor, but I cannot even begin to understand the desperation Aparna is facing.

After a while, Aparna's friend returned after depositing her books in the library. Aparna got up slowly and left with her friend to look for a rickshaw, saying, "Don't tell anyone, Laxman. Bye..."

I watched her leave, feeling so powerless. My usually cheerful friend had left without a smile, with tears in her eyes. She had barely left when Nishant came and said, "Bhaiya, I have to defend my PhD. topic, I need some guidance from you." I said, "Let's go get some tea first." But I was so distressed that I couldn't say much to Nishant. I just took my bike and returned to my room. This ad hoc system has not just destroyed the dreams of many young people, it continues to crush their present and future. If you are an ad hoc professor belonging to a marginalised section of society, the system exploits you in many ways at the same time. And it is only you and your family who face these struggles. The rest of the world has no idea about the difficulties a temporary employee faces!

A very different equation prevails within the campus. Those who are not flexible, don't fit into the system. Governments will take time to change, but these professors change their stripes in no time.

28th February 2017

Professors, Guidebooks and Reports

Suresh told me over the phone that Gangaram Bhadrawaj had been selected at JNU. The interview went like this,

"You're from Political Science. Tell us, what differences do you find between Marx and Lenin?"

"Well, there isn't much of a difference."

Suresh laughed and said that if the interviewer had included Mao too, the answer would have gone from 'isn't much' to 'not a lot'. That night, they felt as if the Vivekananda statue at DU was casting its shadow on the distant statue of Nehru in JNU. They had smiled at each other.

I met Vimala on the Campus, in the afternoon. Vimala was an ad hoc professor like me, teaching in the psychology department of the neighbouring college. She had started teaching three years before me. I didn't know her well, but she was a topper in her college. That's why, the moment she got admission to M.Phil, she was made an ad hoc professor there. She taught with great enthusiasm and was very popular among her students. She had developed unique ways of teaching that made a difficult subject like psychology seem like literature and art. Teaching was her passion. She would carry her laptop and show her class a presentation or a global research paper every week.

But today, she casually mentioned something that left me shocked.

She said, "You know, Laxman, my TIC told me, 'the interview is tomorrow, come over to my place tonight. Consider this a confirmation that you'll be made permanent.'"

"What? Are you serious, Vimala?"

"That is exactly what I'm saying. But who will believe me? Everyone will say I'm lying. But the truth is that this is what happens here."

A few days later, it was known that Vimala had left this field. She had complained, but the principal and several senior professors colluded with each other to suppress the matter. It's said that a senior woman professor used many a ruse to get Vimala's complaint letter back. She said, "You will be defamed because nothing has actually happened." The TIC was sent on leave for a few days, but when he returned, he had written a book and two articles, which got him a promotion. Now he's been made in charge of the 'Gender Sensitivity Cell'.

The old-timers of our department used to tell stories about two professors. Professor Ramkhelawan Tiwari had sent a message to a research scholar, and the girl had complained. The professor was forced to retire. Another professor, Gajodhar Ranjan, did something similar, and the girl told it to everyone in her village in Haryana. The next day, the professor was made to run and was thrashed, the whole way from the Vivekananda statue to the old convocation hall. The professor went to file a report, but when he was asked if he recognised anyone who hit him, he said that they were mostly hitting on his face. A few days later, he got his research institution registered. He went on to write many help books, which professors generally discourage students from buying. He organised one grand seminar after the other. Now he's one of the senior professors and sits on the interview board.

Once Raghu da talked about some past professors of our department, "Professor Jainendra was notorious, for he was a debauch. Today, there are many like him. He had a scooter that was more well-known than him. Professor Jainendra's scooter made many people permanent professors at DU. But look at Ayodhya Singh from JNU, who is even worse. Ayodhya Singh wrote a letter to his brother, who was in BHU, saying, 'The person you recommended for Saugor University doesn't know anything. He couldn't answer even a single question. But since I had promised you, I managed a permanent placement for him. But be careful, don't recommend such people in the future."

"A very different equation prevails within the campus. Those who are not flexible, don't fit into the system. Governments will take time to change, but these professors change their stripes in no time. Yesterday's communists are the first to become Congress supporters. Now most of them are in the Sangh. So many social justice champions have also taken refuge in the Sangh. They're the ones who sit on every selection committee, and mark their presence in every committee. Those who are unable to do so remain just good teachers, living their lives between classes and EMI payments for a house and a car."

Vimala lost her job, but she took with her whatever she could save and went to Mumbai to become a housewife at her husband's home. After that, neither did Vimala ever return, nor did her story.

The walls of the Campus were rapidly **changing colours**.

March 2017

Disturbance during the Seminar

After college, I came to the Campus today. In the Arts faculty, a literary event is being held in room 22. It's been years since any program has been held here. I attended this event, the first to be held since 2012. We had listened to many renowned poets and writers, in this very room. But for some reason, all literary and academic activities had stopped for the last four years. Since 2012, we have been able to experience how a University can function without any seminars and discussions. Every year, lakhs of rupees were allocated for seminars and workshops, but they remained unspent. All activities were at a standstill. But today, the seminar hall is packed. Dozens of professors from various departments, including the Hindi department, are in the audience. Listening to the cultural interpretations of nationalist concerns, it's clear that with a change in power, there will be a change in academic discourse too. Therefore, every academic institution must have a healthy, logical debate on all ideas and ideologies. Vedacharya Munilal Pandey from Banaras is delivering the presidential address.

"Those libraries that question our ancient culture instead of praising it should be set on fire. The biggest problem in India is that, in the desire to be tolerant, we have given excessive liberty to our opponents. Now their ideas have polluted the minds and lifestyles of our youth. Even in these sacred premises of Ma Saraswati, the Goddess of learning, I can see students who have come to acquire knowledge wearing extremely obscene clothes. Film songs are being played at a loud volume. When one is about to be destroyed, one's judgement falters too. These places of education are more sacred than temples. There should be no place for corrupt ideas here."

I was hearing such a lecture for the first time at DU. Meanwhile, at the nearby Shri Krishna College of Commerce, a youth festival, with loud music and dancing, is going on. Just at that moment, the rowdy sounds of girls and boys doing the rain dance to YoYo Honey Singh's songs seem to be mocking Munilal Pandey's speech. But he continues, "We must educate our children in Sanskrit medium. Sanskrit is the language of knowledge and science. Sanskrit is our mother tongue. It is the mother of all languages. How can we be patriots and protectors of culture without teaching our children Sanskrit? The onus of saving them from Western culture is on us."

Suddenly, a researcher asked the Acharya, who is deeply immersed in his worry about the loss of ancient culture, "Sir, do your children also study in a Sanskrit medium school?" Munilal Pandey quickly glanced to see who had interrupted him. He said, "Someone dares to stand in the way of the demonic mentality."

The event has now moved to its second phase, poetry recitation. Suddenly, a fiery voice projects a verse into the audience from the stage,

ahinsa maha sarvottam hai, ye manuj kastooree hai,
dusht agar na smjhe to phir hinsa bahut zaruree hai.

After discussing concerns about academics, the seminar had taken a nationalist turn towards the end. Even senior professors could be seen giving a standing ovation to these verses. Meanwhile, many professors made haste to leave as they had to attend a nationalist seminar on culture, religion, and temple at the conference centre.

The walls of the Campus were rapidly changing colours.

✪ Non-violence is the greatest, it is the treasure of humanity,
but if the wicked don't understand, then violence is necessary.

The girls top the board exams after classes ten and twelve. Their pass percentage is higher than boys. Then where do these girls disappear after class twelve? Why don't they attend degree colleges or universities in the same proportion? Why are the girls pursuing PhD degrees only a quarter of the number of boys doing the same?

April 2017

Where do the professors' children study?

The DUTA rally yesterday was a total flop. Only about 65-70 people turned up. The office bearers had anticipated this therefore they had brought only about a hundred placards. Half of the placards had just come along for the ride and returned to the DUTA office unused. They couldn't find a hand to hold them. The teachers from the South Campus colleges rarely attend such events. Their homes are too far away, spreading from Dwarka to Vasundhara. To participate in the DUTA rally and return home by 3 pm means getting stuck in the hours-long traffic jams at the Noida toll and at Dhaulakuan. The teachers have smartly avoided DUTA's rallies and saved themselves from Delhi's traffic chaos. The category of people who think 'if everyone benefits, we will benefit too, otherwise what we're getting is enough' usually stay away from protests and demonstrations. And here is DUTA, which habitually causes traffic jams, every month, from Mandi House to Jantar-Mantar.

When only a few people turned up for the rally yesterday, it was wrapped up quickly. As always, the list of issues on the DUTA banner was a jumble, with problems of ad hoc teachers and permanent teachers vying with those of the pensioners. I turned up for the rally but when I saw that only a few ad hoc teachers had turned up, I left to get the magazine from the nearby NSD. When I returned, a speaker was addressing a small group of around ten people, lamenting how higher education had gone to the dogs. I have acquired a taste for the samosas at the Mandi House canteen opposite Himachal Bhavan. I remember when Amarendra sir first treated me to one in 2015. It had tasted quite bland.

I don't spend much time in the staff room anymore. I usually rush after taking my class. Nowadays, everyone is making Ad hoc teachers a target. I have a little time before my next class, and take another cup of green tea. With each sip, I can hear the gossip around me.

"You know, Ragini Ma'am, DUTA doesn't do anything. I was appointed in 2006 and I'm still an assistant professor. Look at Raksha, she was my batchmate. She became permanent three years after me and is an associate professor now in Gwalior. Honestly, DUTA shouldn't be allowed to exist anymore. There's no life left in it. They only do dirty politics."

"Absolutely, Sonika, that's why I never attended a DUTA rally. You used to be so eager to attend them. Now you have understood. From the beginning, I knew that they only do politics. And you know I hate politics."

"Yes, ma'am, you're right. I only went to the DUTA rallies twice or thrice. Since my children grew up, I've been focused on them. Aarav is going to the sixth class now."

"Both my children are settled. Ankush didn't like Australia, now he's going to Denmark. Nilesh has been calling me to Belgium for ages now."

"Exactly, and anyway, higher education in this country is terrible."

I'm listening to this conversation in the staff room of a college at Delhi University. All of these people are professors. But their children don't study at the universities where their parents teach, because they know the reality. The reality of the way they teach and of the system. They don't want to spoil the future of their children. Who would knowingly educate their child in such a system?

Just then Aparna called. She said that she had been expelled from college. The administration asked her to choose between her job and having a child. Although Aparna had to inform the college in writing that she was unable to take classes due to her approaching delivery. But the college administration did what they shouldn't have done. They fired Aparna from her ad hoc job. Aparna said,

"I don't ever want my daughter to feel that her mother lost her job before she was born."

Has someone ever raised this question about the education system? The girls top the board exams after classes ten and twelve. Their pass percentage is higher than boys. Then where do these girls disappear after class twelve? Why don't they attend degree colleges or universities in the same proportion? Why are the girls pursuing PhD degrees only a quarter of the number of boys doing the same? Government documents do not reflect people's shattered dreams. They are only about numbers and statistics.

Human existence has been reduced to mere numbers.

I've struggled hard to get here.

I will somehow continue my studies.

I don't have a choice, sir.

July 2017

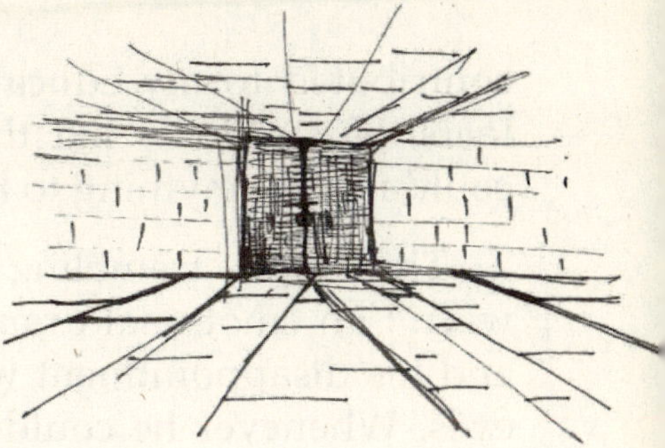

Shutting Doors in the Face

Today was the last day for the second cutoff list at Delhi University. A boy named Rajesh from Nuh, Haryana, came to me. He looked anxious. His score was just one per cent less than the cutoff percentage. He asked, "Sir, Will I make it to the next cutoff list?" When I said it might not be possible since the OBC seats were almost full, his eyes welled up with tears. I put my hand on his shoulder and said, "Rajesh, try another college, you'll get admission somewhere surely, don't worry." He began speaking in a trembling voice, and I listened quietly. He said,

"Sir, I'm the first boy from my village to pass class twelve. I have come here to study as I have the best marks. I saw that the fee is nominal in your college, therefore I collected money from many people to pay it. I've already tried many colleges. If I don't get admission, my family will be devastated, and no one will ever send their child to Delhi again. People will stop educating their children. Sir, it's just one per cent less, please consider it. What will I tell everyone when I go back? Everyone has contributed to my education." Trying to stop his tears, he suddenly left the room. I felt helpless I could not do anything to help him.

The boy's trembling voice revealed that it wasn't an emotional drama. His shattered dreams and his disappointment were bringing tears to his eyes. Whenever he could not control his tears, he would leave the room. I asked if he had come with someone, and he said he had come alone. His worn-out clothes, dog-eared documents, and trembling legs revealed that despite his best efforts, his dreams had been defeated by numbers. We have created a system where immense courage is often sacrificed at the altar of marks.

It was three pm. As I was leaving, I saw him sitting quietly in a corner of the college, amidst the chaos of the admission process. I went to him, and said, "Don't worry, son, you'll surely get admission somewhere. Everything in DU is based on merit, we can't do anything." He said, "It's okay, sir. I'll wait for the next cutoff list. If that doesn't work out, I'll think of something else. I've struggled hard to get here. I will somehow continue my studies.

I don't have a choice, sir."

The pen and the book were always free, but sometimes royal courts and at other times governments tried to enslave them.

Common people wrote history on a grey slate with a reed pen.

August 2017

The non-teaching staff on the Campus

There has never been a golden age in higher education. The pen and the book were always free, but sometimes royal courts and at other times governments tried to enslave them. Common people wrote history on a grey slate sometimes with a mango stem, other times with a reed pen. All over the country, higher education is going through its worst phase. It hasn't been a particular government or one party that has pushed it into this darkness. Everyone has a hand in it, some less, some more.

An independent India dreamed of building good universities, but they are crumbling from within now, and from outside, they are being propped up to stop their collapse. One such prop is the NAAC (National Assessment and Accreditation Council). NAAC is an institution that evaluates the academic quality and related criteria of an institution and grades them accordingly. The NAAC team is coming to our college. The entire college has been decorated. Like always, as soon as I entered gate number two on my bike, Mujeeb, standing at the gate, said, "Sir, today parking will be via the back gate. The team is coming today, isn't it?" I said, "Okay." Then, as I was leaving, Mujeeb asked, "Sir, will the team talk only to the teaching staff? Or also to the non-teaching staff?"

"I have no idea, but why do you want to know?"

Because nobody cares about us. We are moved from one duty to another. No one talks about our issues at all. Sometimes the Principal does listen to us. We have never even met the VC, he doesn't know us nor do we know him. Yet, we are a part of the university too, but only in name. Therefore, I thought to ask you to introduce us to the team today. We will tell them our grievances. Now, it is becoming difficult to do our job, sir."

Mujeeb Chacha smiles and greets us with such warmth, as if he were a relative, and opens the main gate every day. I always stop and ask about his well-being. Today, Mujeeb kept talking and I listened. Maybe he thought that if he told me, something would happen. As if I am some big-shot guy.

Parcham

21st September, 2017

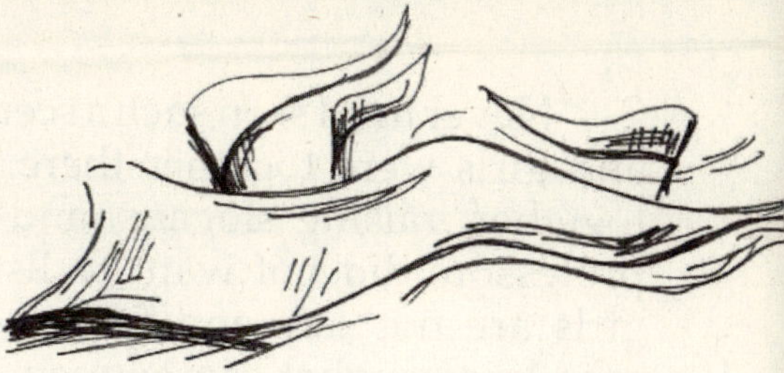

Waving their Aanchals like Pennants

It was a landmark day for the central universities of the country. Today, the girls of Banaras Hindu University (BHU) protested against the discrimination on their Campus, the restrictive timings imposed on them in their hostels and the harassment they face on the roads every day. Hundreds of girls blocked the main gate of BHU, in Lanka. It was the first time that most of these girls participated in a protest or demonstration, without even informing their families. They were singing:

> tere kandhe pe ye aanchl bahut khoob hai lekin,
> tum is aanchl ko parcham bana leti to achchha tha.

The police used batons to disperse the protesting girls at the BHU gate. This was the first time such a student protest was taking place in 'Mahamana ki Bagia'. And it was ironic that the police were trying to suppress them only. Radhika was injured too. After her post-graduation from DU, she could not get admission to a PhD program. That is why she is doing her PhD at BHU. She told me over the phone:

✪ Your aanchal looks good on your shoulder, but wouldn't it be better if you made it a pennant.

"Never had I seen such a scene. Hundreds of boys and girls were together there. They were fighting together, raising slogans, and singing songs. Our professors did not want to listen to us. When we girls are not safe and free even on our Campus, who knows what can happen outside? My mother was also a victim of a lathi charge in Lucknow this month. She works in an Anganwadi centre and was sitting in protest over her demands. My brother lives in Chhota Baghada and is preparing for his SSC. Everyone in my family studies or works away from home and they understand the situation. But after seeing my friend Priyanka's photo in the newspaper, her family took her home."

Once, the girls at Allahabad University had protested in the same way. The boys' hostel at Allahabad University was as famous for producing IAS and PCS officers as it was for making bombs and having gang wars. The student union building behind the statue of the martyr Lal Padmadhar was a landmark of Allahabad University. People from Chota Baghada, Chandpur Salori, Govindpur, Allapur and Daraganj as well as George Town and Civil Lines, come together in one campus. A university builds a city. It also brings about changes in the city and society. A university must have more power than the city. If the City tries to dominate, the campus will not be able to take it.

Whether it's Allahabad University or BHU, they were trying to be a beacon, ahead of their time. But when did the city absorb these campuses, it isn't clear. The shortcomings of these two cities were carried over to the campuses.

Now the cities lead, and the universities are following.

Generations upon generations have been paying the price, we were preparing ourselves to hold everyone to account.

8th December 2017

URDF: A Successful Attempt

It has been five years since I shifted to Gandhi Vihar. I have a 10×10 foot room with a separate kitchen and a veranda. The rent is high because it has a park-facing view. For us, that is all friends from DU, JNU and Jamia, this is our adda, our place to hang out and chill. We sit here and hold long discussions on topics like – What is a campus? How can one encourage debate, dialogue and discussion inside a campus? My cook, Dhrup Kumar had understood that there would be a few social thinkers at my place each evening, which for him translated to a few extra people to feed.

One evening, we discussed the absence of seminars or gatherings at DU. Nothing except sponsored programs were taking place. Programs on religion, the Ram temple, and Hindutva have already taken place in the conference centre. Therefore, it was decided that researchers and professors should organise some people-centred events together. They should include topics related to literature, society, and politics. There should be two or three speakers and also a question-answer session. To begin, people from all universities in Delhi should be invited. Once the event is successful, researchers and professors from other campuses in the country will also be invited. We started study circles, group discussions, and some social programs on our campus with the help of dialogue forums like URDF.

We created a team. We didn't even try to get a room or a hall for our programs because it wouldn't have been available. The first meeting was called on the campus, in front of the Vivekananda statue on the Dhruv Mistry lawn. The topic today is - Dr. Ambedkar and the India of today. There are three speakers, all from central universities. The audience is from both within and outside the campus.

When we found that the university was far from what we had dreamed and imagined, a few passionate people like us began shaping and colouring whatever we could to our specifications. In this study circle, we had some brilliant seminars on subjects ranging from Kabir, Phule, the question of Pasmanda, Phoolan Devi, and Ramashankar Yadav Vidrohi to various literary and cultural issues. At one point, around 150 people participated in them. It filled the emptiness of the Campus with so much hope.

After returning to my flat in the evening, I filed an online RTI application. I wanted to know the number of SC, ST and OBC professors, vice-chancellors and employees in central universities across the country, from the UGC. I got the answer a few days later.

There is not even one OBC professor in 45 of the central universities of the country. The number of SC and ST professors is negligible. The UGC refused to provide data on vice-chancellors, saying that the post is a single position and therefore reservation is not applicable. I prepared a formal report on this RTI and made it public.

This became the most viral news at the time. Later, some figures from someone else's RTI application were widely publicised on social media. According to that, out of 596 vice-chancellors, 6 are SC, 6 are ST, and 36 are OBC. The rest are all from higher castes. Even seven decades after Independence, universities were not inclusive, and all were not welcomed equally on campuses. This realisation started bothering us. In our newfound awareness, we wrote articles, gathered data through RTI applications, and made people cognisant of the facts. In short, I had taken to writing to express this self-awareness. I was unaware that this fight for rights and justice would threaten my academic career, and that I would have to pay the price in the future.

Generations upon generations have been paying the price, we were preparing ourselves to hold everyone to account.

Ignoring his words,
I moved f o r w a r d .

5th March 2018

The matter of the Roster

As far as social justice is concerned, today is the cruellest day for higher education. The UGC has issued an order for a change of roster in the universities. In simple terms, the 200-point roster has been replaced with a 13-point roster. The impact of this notification will be that those from deprived and marginalised communities will have little or no chance to become professors in universities.

A roster is the systematic order of reserved positions which came into being after the implementation of reservation in higher education. It is an organised sequence of all approved positions, guaranteeing 15% SC, 7.5% ST, and 27% OBC positions.

Reservation was implemented in higher education after decades of struggle. The SCs and STs got reservations in the 90s, and OBCs in 2007. Initially, various kinds of rosters were made - the 40-point roster, the L-shape roster, and the department-wise 13-point roster. Later, after a long long struggle came the 200-point roster. The UGC, counting the University as one unit, changed the present 200-point roster to the department-wise 13-point roster. The direct impact of this decision would have been that reserved category positions would be almost negligible during appointments to the post of professor.

Last year, a research scholar from BHU filed a petition in the Allahabad High Court. In response, the court ordered the implementation of a department-wise roster. The order was challenged in the Supreme Court, which upheld it.

Based on that, the UGC has implemented the department-wise roster today. It's not so difficult to understand the casteist conspiracy behind this decision. That evening, I tried to understand the roster system from many people in the DU office. No one could explain it in simple terms beyond basic information. Everyone agreed that it was a very complex issue. Jitendra Chauhan sir, a professor at my college said, "Prof. Milind Babu from the English department has a good understanding of reservation-related matters. In the fight for reservation at Court, he's one of the big names. Meet him."

I telephoned Professor Milind Babu. Scholars and professors like him are the very backbone of a university. I met him on the North Campus. We talked for a long time. He explained the roster to me in simple terms. Now, we had to explain it to the whole country. He suggested I read a book, which I found at 'Jain Book Depot', in the Inner Circle of

Rajiv Chowk, after looking for it all around Delhi. That evening, I read the important portions and took notes. I felt that it was the need of the hour to mount a united movement on the roster issue. I wrote a long post on Facebook to explain my take on it.

At 10 pm that night, a senior professor called me. He spoke politely, "There are so many permanent employees in DU, but they are silent. What's your problem? Why are you writing about this controversial issue so openly? You should remain silent. First, secure a permanent position for yourself. Then do this."

I became worried. His concern was justified. But we weren't doing anything wrong. Ignoring his words, I moved forward.

Whose hands they were...

6th March 2018

The Script of the Roster Movement

The teachers from the Bahujan community held a meeting at the DUTA office today. The hall was packed. It was decided that we need to take to the streets on the roster issue. This decision, based on casteism, has been taken under the guise of a Supreme Court order. People are angry on this issue and we need to organise this anger into a movement. It was decided that we would not tolerate this social injustice. The teachers' union has also called an emergency meeting in the next one or two days.

Associate Professor Gajraj, who used to fight for many issues as a student but is given to swinging like a pendulum in the politics of the teachers' union now, said, "When the first opportunity arose for Dalits, backward classes, and tribals to become professors, they wanted to block our path. But we are not going to stop now. We'll sound the battle drum."

Chaman Lal, Associate Professor at Birsa Munda College, has been fighting for social justice since the very beginning. In today's meeting, he said, "I want to say this to the Bahujan professors all over the country: Come out of your comfort zone! They're not giving me a promotion; they have filed a case instead. I did not feel afraid; I'm fighting all alone. Now, let's all fight together. If not, we might as well return to the village and graze buffalos. This fight needs to be a do-or-die fight."

Divyanshu Kumar, from Swami Sehajanand College, is the Vice President of DUTA. He said, "We understand why this roster has been changed. They don't want us, the first-generation people from backward and deprived classes, to be a part of this system. We need to tell people all over the country how this government has changed the roster under the guise of the Supreme Court order. This fight will now spread from DU to the whole country."

The meeting continued with many speakers expressing their views and voicing their support for the movement. Later, we agreed that everyone would put aside their affiliations to respective parties and organisations. We would unite for the sake of the Constitution and social justice. All joined the roster movement, ditching our political leanings and status, right-wing or left-wing, socialists or social justice activists, researchers, students, or professors. This was becoming a people's movement.

For my part, I chose to help demystify the complexities and intricacies of the roster in simple language. I wrote dozens of articles, collected data, and created charts and graphics. Many friends from DU and JNU did the same and it came out came out brilliantly. We regularly held meetings. The URDF team had already laid the foundation by combining the ideologies of Birsa, Phule, Ambedkar, Periyar, and Bhagat Singh. That team took on the lead in this movement. Some would make posters, others would connect with people, some met with MPs, and others handled the media.

In the coming days, the roster movement became a mass movement.

Amid this preparation, while strolling in the North Campus one evening, we met our senior professor, Parmeshwar Singh. He said with great familiarity, "Look, Laxman, protesting is our civic duty. But I want to know whether you have a job in Bihar?"

"Yes, sir! I got a job at Tilka Manjhi University, Bhagalpur. But I didn't join. I let it go. I'll stay here in my beloved DU. This is my university."

"Oh! Why did you make such a big mistake? You should prioritise your career. You're at the forefront of this movement, and your speeches are impressive. You speak from the heart and tell the truth, but this will cause you great harm. Most people here are permanent employees. Nothing will happen to them.This isn't the Congress era, where even the Sanghis were given jobs under some pretext. When the interviews start taking place here, they'll selectively throw out those who have been speaking up. And look at you, you've let go of your permanent job in Bihar."

"You are right to be concerned, sir. Thank you for the warmth and good wishes. But it has been ten years since I have been teaching at DU. Where else will I find such an academic environment, sir? I will find a permanent placement here only. My merit is good. If nowhere else, then my present college is not bad too. Many people care for me and they will ensure that I am treated fairly."

"You are under a big illusion. I am saying this to you because you have been my student. When you had submitted your Ph.D., I was the head of the department. I am worried about you. You are so honest and true. Not everyone appreciates those qualities."

"Sir, if I don't speak up today for fear of losing my job, it will kill me. I will fall in my own eyes. Professors like you have taught me the importance of having principles."

"You are first-generation teachers from a backward and deprived background. You have a lot to lose. No one will come to wipe your tears. Take up the job in Bihar for now, you can return to DU later when the time is right. Abhijnan Prakash, and Ranuj, all have left, right? Aren't they working elsewhere? The rest is up to you."

"Sir! If you don't mind, you also had numerous opportunities."

"You are correct. We are guilty. Despite being here, we could not secure a permanent placement for students like you. I regret it. But now you also understand the system, right? Everything wasn't entirely up to us. These hands are trying to keep higher education in place. It was too late before we figured out whose hands they were and who held them."

Repeal the 13-point roster!

Inqilab Zindabad!

Student-Teacher Unity Zindaabad!

Jai Jai Jai Jai Jai Bheem!

15th March 2018

Jai Bheem in the Teacher's Movement

DUTA has organised a protest march today from Mandi House to Parliament Street. Teachers and students from DU, JNU, AUD and hundreds of other campuses nationwide, have gathered. The rally began at Mandi House and moved towards Parliament Street via Barakhamba Road. Today, for the first time, I witnessed an unusual scene. Amidst the chants of "Inqilab Zindabad!", "Student-Teacher Unity Zindaabad!", and "DUTA March On!", a new slogan emerged - "Jai Jai Jai Jai Jai Bheem!"

I had never heard this slogan at DUTA before, despite its significance after the Rohith Vemula movement. Today, Rupendra Chaudhary sir began chanting it, followed by many of our Bahujan professors. Then, Rupendra Chaudhary sir handed me the microphone. I was excited. I expanded the reach of this slogan:

The slaying of social justice will never be tolerated!

Repeal the 13-point roster!

The scene I saw today was new to me. For the first time, prominent leaders from higher caste-led teachers' organisations raised the 'Jai Bheem' slogan. The first major rally regarding the roster movement was a success today because of our efforts.

Professors, whether permanent or ad hoc, were present in considerable numbers. Everyone spoke with one voice: the circular of 5th March must be withdrawn at all costs! All teachers' organisations and other teachers labelled it as anti-reservation. Sanjeev Roy, the DUTA President, stated, "First and foremost, I want to clarify that this is the DUTA of 2018, not the DUTA of 1990. Times have changed. We will fight for social justice and win at any cost. DUTA will fight this battle with all its might."

It sounded like a new history was being written. This statement indicated that while DUTA had made mistakes regarding social justice and reservation in 1990 and later, they would not be repeated. There was no doubt that anti-reservation views have dominated the universities in the country. But the times have changed. Today's march brought together advocates of social justice from right-wing, and left-wing organisations and the Congress party. The roster movement has made the boundaries of organisations fluid for some time.

The roster movement is a litmus test for how successfully our constitution has been implemented on the ground level after seven decades of Independence.

How could I tell the students about such incidents?

How could I tell them that the exam that determines their fate, in a way, is taken so casually by some irresponsible people?

Why lower their morale?

28th April 2018

Saying what is False and Hiding what isTrue.

Today is the final class of BA Third Year. In the final class, professors generally act like preachers. The students said, "Sir, the course has been completed. Revision is over. Please give us some advice for the future."

I told them, "First, read the question paper carefully. Begin with the question you can answer best. Make sure no questions are overlooked. Keep your answer sheet neat and organised because it will represent you before the examiner. He will not see you, only your work. And yes! The examiner is someone whom you have never met before and will never meet again, therefore present yourself as best as possible..."

I was about to say more but stopped suddenly. These things should not be said in front of students. One gets around twenty-five rupees for correcting an answer sheet. Altogether, it makes five or seven hundred rupees per bundle. Arun told me the other day that many people have earned as much as half the value of their flats from this. Ranjan Kumar, from your college, is the top answer sheet evaluator in the university. He holds a record of checking twelve bundles in a day, which is documented in the University Book of Records. Those who cannot answer the students' questions in the classroom, check answer sheets quickly. That's why the university has a rule that three persons will check an answer sheet to ensure a fair evaluation.

Once, my co-examiner brought a fifth bundle for checking. Showing him an answer sheet from the second bundle, I asked, "Sir! You have marked this student in twice, although he has written the identical answer twice in different places."

"Oh! Is that so? Never mind, Laxman. At least he made an effort to write it twice. Give him the marks."

How could I tell the students about such incidents? How could I tell them that the exam that determines their fate, in a way, is taken so casually by some irresponsible people? Why lower their morale? So, in the last class of the course, I bolstered their spirits by saying, "Become a more aware, intelligent and understanding person. You have got this opportunity, not everyone gets it. Study hard; it will free you from whatever bogs you down."

"One of the students asked, "Sir, it's my last semester. Which field should I pursue next? What should I prepare for?"

"Whatever you're interested in. By the way, what would you like to do?"

"I want to become a professor, sir. From where should I do my MA? And do tell me more about the NET-JRF. I'll do it simultaneously with MA."

I couldn't figure out how to answer this question. That student's face reminded me of a younger version of myself from my undergraduate and postgraduate years. My student wants to become a professor and I've been teaching on an ad hoc basis for the past nine years. I met all the eligibility criteria for a permanent placement the day I joined the ad hoc position. After more than two dozen interviews, I'm still an ad hoc professor. The student I taught for three years has asked me for advice on becoming a professor! This is the most disheartening question of my academic career. I could have talked about anything else for hours, but today I was speechless. I told him about the rules and regulations of MA, NET-JRF, and PhD I tried to encourage him. But…

Jai Bheem!

Jai Mandal!

Jai Samvidhan!

31st January 2019

We will have the Roster!

It is a landmark day for the Roster Movement. On January 29, the court rejected the central government's plea for the roster for the third time. By then, the Roster Movement had spread to the villages. We had an emergency meeting at DU yesterday and decided to hold an 'Akrosh March' from Mandi House to Jantar Mantar today. In the morning, a senior police officer called me,

"Are you Dr. Laxman Yadav? I am calling from Sansad Marg police station."

"Yes, This is me. Please tell me."

"Have you all started doing politics too? Professors should focus only on teaching and learning. They should stay away from politics. What's the need for all this?"

"Okay, sir, tell me one thing. Who makes all the decisions about our teaching and learning?"

"Your VC and the Education Department."

"Who appoints the VC and how do they do so? Politics does, right? This politics also determines who gets the opportunity to become a professor and who doesn't. Isn't it a citizen's responsibility to speak up against what's wrong? And if speaking up against something wrong is political, shouldn't you be doing the same?"

"Okay, if this is what happens, then it's unacceptable. Alright, we will fully support you, Laxman bhai! I agree with what you're saying. By the way, how many people are expected to come and what is the program for the day?"

"There's no estimate of the number of people, and the program ahead is to struggle."

A part of the Barakhamba road gradually filled up with flags, banners, and posters of organisations. People were participating in large numbers, not only from Delhi but also from other cities. This New Delhi area echoed with slogans such as 'Jai Bheem!', 'Jai Mandal!', 'Jai Samvidhan!', drumbeats and claps. It was a wonderful sight! To see university campuses in India awakened to justice and their rights! Except for one party, all major social organisations and political parties that believed in the Constitution and social justice made their way to Jantar Mantar.

This parade of justice-loving citizens arrived at Jantar Mantar. It was an unforgettable sight for me.

I don't know where I'm not sure where I found the strength to shout out the slogans -

to kaun sa wala, roster?
ambedkar wala roster!
to lohiya wala roster!
phule wala roster!
savitree wala roster!
mndl wala roster!
snvidhan wala roster!
hum le ke rahenge roster!

jo tum na doge roster to chheen ke lenge roster!

Listen, O Manuwadi!

Now the time has changed. We will now create a Campus that values justice and is inclusive. If you support us, we'll let you follow **US**.

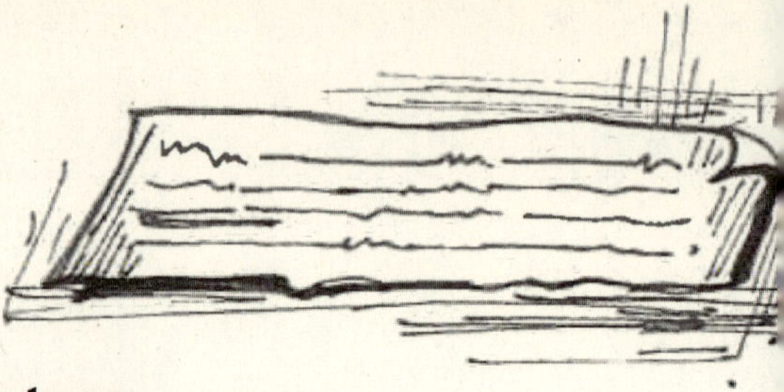

5th March 2019

To Create History, Remember History

The unified platform formed for the Roster Movement has called for a 'Bharat Bandh' today. A fight for rights beginning at a university has escalated to a Bharat Bandh, which is a landmark event in India over the last decade. The Roster Movement has spread to villages and small towns. Pictures of roadblocks began coming in from several states. Videos with the slogan 'Take back the 13-point roster' have gone viral on social media from villages to big cities. Today, another march will go from Mandi House to Jantar Mantar. We had to work quite hard to get the backing of DUTA (Delhi University Teachers' Association). The efforts of the then-president Sanjeev Ray, Vice-president Divyanshu Kumar and several professors have borne fruit.

Professor Gajraj is speaking. "Tell me, when Delhi University has been making the roster since 2013, the shortfalls and backlogs were resolved, and the BJP was not there then. Who were those people who took the hundreds of SC, ST, and OBC seats?

Who were those who repeatedly said NFS (Non-Fulfillment of Seats) on reserved seats? Who went to court and challenged reservation? They were the same people whose way of thinking had turned DU into a hotbed of anti-Mandal sentiments. The DU had resisted social justice by creating a 'Kranti Chowk' (Revolution Square). Now the times have changed. We will now create a Campus that values justice and is inclusive. If you support us, we'll let you follow us. You're all educated; rise above your caste interests. Become more human. Times are changing. Come, let us walk ahead together."

People like Professor Gajraj remember the past while creating new history. Now, a common history is being written. God knows how many people worked so hard to make this happen. Today's Bharat Bandh was successful. Along with Delhi University students, researchers, and professors, lakhs of people have joined to make it a mass movement. By the evening, social media was flooded with photos and videos of the Bharat Bandh from around the country. The people of villages and small towns became the movement's strongest supporters. The central government has perhaps understood that it must pass an ordinance.

The collective struggle of India's farmers, workers, and ordinary citizens had made history.

7 March, 2019

An Ordinance on the Roster

By the evening of the Bharat Bandh, we could see the results of our efforts. The collective struggle of India's farmers, workers, and ordinary citizens had made history. The protesters experience a sense of victory. The final cabinet meeting before the general elections will be held today. We have gathered in and around the DUTA office. According to certain sources, the government was to bring an ordinance on the 200-point roster in today's meeting. Nothing could be confirmed before the ordinance was issued.

My friends and I began to recollect events of the movement that had been going on for a whole year. Everyone had their own story about the movement.

"Initially, I wondered whether the university professors, who are so afraid for their jobs, would participate in this movement. However, a large number of them came. That's where the whole thing began."

"However, the Bahujans have more organisations than leaders. I was afraid they might start fighting among themselves. But everyone banded together and fought against the regime. Social organisations and activists took the protest to the villages. Almost every student organisation supported it. That is why we were able to fight."

"We all must agree on one thing, none of this would have been possible without social media. The news channels covered barely anything. Social media is the true media."

"We must remember this. In the Parliament, leaders of all opposition parties including SP, BSP, RJD, AAP, Congress, DMK and the Communist parties supported us. We were able to prevail because it became a political fight."

Then Abhijyan Prakash chuckled and added, "Do you remember what happened when we went to the house of the ruling party MP Baldev Narayan? We began explaining to him - 'Sir, the government has changed the roster. Previously, it was a 200-point roster, now they want to change to the 13-point one, which will result in a significant loss for the reserved seats."

"He said, 'Wait, let's say there are two seats. If one went to the general category, who gets the second seat? SC, ST, or OBC?"

"We replied, 'No sir, the roster doesn't work like that. Previously, It was a 200-point one, now they are introducing a 13-point one…"

"He replied, 'No, no, leave this thirteen-fourteen. Tell me, if there are two posts, one goes to the general category, who gets the second seat?"

"Just then, the DUTA Vice President Divyanshu Kumar arrived. As soon as he came, he said, 'Wait, Laxman, let me explain.'"

"You told him, 'No sir, this man is fixated on one thing. He will not understand.'"

"Divyanshu Kumar retorted, 'We have explained the roster system to the whole country, why can't we explain it to him?'"

"Addressing the MP, Divyanshu Kumar said, 'See, sir, the real issue is that the government does not recognise that a massive injustice is taking place. This is the first time that Dalits, backwards classes and tribals have come close to becoming academics in this country. Earlier it was a 200-point roster, now they are changing it to a 13-point one, which will...'"

"The MP became agitated, '13-point again... whoever comes gets stuck on 13! Bhai, just tell me, of the two posts, who will get the second one?"

"We all got up without even drinking a glass of water. While leaving, Divyanshu Kumar suddenly asked, 'Who suggested coming to his house?' The person who suggested coming to Baldev ji's house quietly slipped away first."

"Sir, what is the point of blaming these leaders? My Babuji commented just today that everyone is getting jobs easily enough. Only these people are complaining about the roster. Getting all worked up about nothing! They've fallen into the trap of the communists. The Prime Minister can do no wrong."

Everyone burst out laughing. Everyone has their own stories and their memories. Meanwhile, the cabinet meeting began. We were following ANI's news coverage. A little while later, the breaking news flashed. The government has passed the ordinance in the cabinet. Our hard work paid off. History has been made. Later, when the copy of the ordinance arrived, the euphoria multiplied. OBCs have also been given reservations for Associate Professor and Professor posts now.

The same slogans were raised again in front of the Vivekananda statue.

'So, which roster?
Ambedkar's roster!
Lohia's roster!
Phule's roster!
Savitri's roster!
Mandal's roster!
Constitution's roster!'

When I arrived at my college, G.K. Didosia commented, "How are you, Netaji? Now you should think of contesting in the elections."

"Thank you, sir. Congratulations, by the way!"

"What congratulations, I'm not bothered. I believe that there should be no reservation at all in education. What about merit then? It is preferable to waive the fees and provide free books and notebooks, but reservation should be based solely on economic criteria. This is like giving away crutches for free."

"Never you mind, sir. You just enjoy the laddus; I won't waste my time explaining and correcting you. Even the Constitution couldn't do this job, now only time will teach you. Get well soon, sir."

Didosia isn't alone. Most professors in higher education still hold this kind of view about reservation and social justice."

☆ A central university in Maharashtra suspended several students for reportedly celebrating 'Manyavar Kanshi Ram Jayanti' on campus. On the same day, ☆ A professor of the English department at DU's North Campus was pursued and beaten up by goons from a government-backed student organisation.

October 2019

Our Times need a Filter

A video has been going viral on social media since morning. The atmosphere inside university campuses is changing rapidly. Everyone feels it. Everyone is either a part of this change or adapting themselves to it. The Vice Chancellor of Purvanchal University is currently trending on social media. In a program, the Vice Chancellor warns, "If you lose a fight with someone outside campus, don't come crying to me. Destroy your adversary first and then come. Whatever happens after that, your Vice Chancellor will handle it. You are the bold and fearless students of Purvanchal University."

While returning from college, I went to the North Campus. A friend has to submit his PhD. Researchers get scholarships erratically now, not every month like before. The UGC says there are no funds. You will get it when the fund arrives. So many fellowships are stopped like this and people usually don't even get to know.

The mood at North Campus has become frenetic due to the impending student union elections. All campus roads are chock-a-block with expensive cars and the walls are plastered with posters. Despite being in the same city, the student unions at DU and JNU are very different. Once, Jitendra Chauhan sir said, "JNU is an island. It has been unable to connect with the outside world. I wish JNU could reach out beyond its boundaries!"

When I studied at Allahabad University, I realised how important student unions are. Student union politics is like a nursery for a diverse and vibrant democracy. However, they are deliberately shut down or allowed to go to ruin.

Meanwhile, a central university in Maharashtra suspended several students for reportedly celebrating 'Manyavar Kanshi Ram Jayanti' on campus. On the same day, a professor of the English department at DU's North Campus was pursued and beaten up by goons from a government-backed student organisation.

A story concerning the Vice Chancellor of an old central university in UP has gone viral. He has been accused of taking crores of rupees for permanent appointments. The Vice Chancellor's son has established his own degree college.

Interviews for permanent positions are going to begin at DU. I attended today's staff council meeting at the college and sat silently, as usual, like the other ad hoc teachers who come to these meetings solely to mark their presence. Nowadays, there is some hustle-bustle at these meetings. There is a charged atmosphere on every campus. Controversies are growing.

After the meeting, I accompanied Mohammad Tauqeer Anwar to the area where a few people came to smoke. Today, Tauqeer ji shared an incredible story.

"It was while Mohammad Aslam Junaid sahab was the principal. After a staff council meeting like this, a Maulana professor approached him and said, 'Sir, I have a request.'

'Yes, please tell me.'

'Many people smoke cigarettes behind the staff room, and the smoke blows in this direction. You should do something about it.'

After some thought, Junaid sahab replied, 'If you want, we can install an exhaust fan there.' And he smiled and left.

Muhammad Aslam Junaid sahab took everyone along with him. Today, in the same college, our students are fighting with each other over whether or not non-veg food can be served at a college party. And all this is taking place inside our own college. As for the atmosphere outside, it is extremely heated, my friend."

While taking the last puff, the burnt part of his cigarette fell off. Tauqeer Anwar was so caught up in his memories, that he didn't notice the cigarette had run out. He gazed at the filter left in his hand. Throwing it away, he said,

"Our era needs a filter too."

The DU VC office, or the Vice Regal Hall, was previously the residence of the Viceroy of British India. It was this building in whose basement Bhagat Singh was detained for three days following his arrest. I had entered that building for the first time in ten years. Only one slogan was raised repeatedly there:

Inquilab Zindabad!

4th December 2019

Where Shaheed-e-Azam was Imprisoned

DU teachers are demonstrating today against the Vice Chancellor for removing thousands of ad hoc professors from their jobs. Thousands of ad hoc teachers, permanent teachers and students are participating in the protest. Slogans were shouted at Gate No. 4 for a while. Nobody has any idea what will happen next. It has become a routine for the whole Maurice Nagar police station to camp inside the DU campus during any protest or rally. Today, paramilitary forces and police from several other stations have also been called in, as if the faculty and students of the university were not protesting against their own Vice Chancellor but were carrying out a terrorist attack.

There was a time when the Vice Chancellor of a central university wrote a letter to the President and had a police captain fired for sending police inside the campus without the Vice Chancellor's permission.

Thousands of people gathered in front of the gate opposite Gate No. 4 and have now moved towards the Vice Chancellor's office. Ajay Singh, a security officer stands behind the security guards employed on a contract basis. Ironically, ad hoc security guards have been deployed to stop the protest of ad hoc professors. This is a conspiracy of the regime. It is most convenient for the king when his subjects fight among themselves. In this instance, who will point fingers at the king?

The protesters reach the gate. They attempt to open it to convey their dissatisfaction to the Vice Chancellor. On the other side, Ajay Singh warns the guards, "If anyone moves away from the security gate, they will be fired. Under no circumstances should the gate be opened."

The contract security guards, who signed a contract for twenty thousand rupees but were only paid between eight and ten thousand, were being intimidated from behind. The contract guards could not contain the rage of the ad hoc teachers. The gate is broken. Thousands of teachers reach the Vice Chancellor's office. The Vice Chancellor is absent and they take control of the Vice Chancellor's office. Such scenes have not been witnessed in the history of independent India. No university in the country has so many ad hoc teachers, such a strong teachers' union, or the advantage of being in the national capital. As a result, they cannot vent their anger or raise their voices because no one is listening to them. Today, five thousand ad hoc DU teachers, and DUTA members took control of the Vice Chancellor's office.

The DU VC office, or the Vice Regal Hall, was previously the residence of the Viceroy of British India. It was this building in whose basement Bhagat Singh was detained for three days following his arrest. I had entered that building for the first time in ten years. Only one slogan was raised repeatedly there: Inquilab Zindabad!

The Vice Chancellor's office had been taken over. Many ad hoc professors are now speaking up. Those who were earlier afraid of being punished for speaking up, are now shouting. When people are repeatedly threatened, they overcome their fears and become fearless.

Today is a historic day, not only for DU but for all the campuses in the country. The Vice-Chancellor is not in, and thousands of teachers have taken control of the entire office.

I wish such a day hadn't come!

I wish such days and such scenes take place on every campus!

The difference between these two statements is the real reason for the decline of higher education.

The situation has changed so much that those who previously opposed universities becoming political hubs are now being political in the name of those institutions.

15th December 2019

Tear Gas Shells in the Library

How could I convince anyone that universities are an 'age of time'? Another country. It is the responsibility of its citizens to ensure it is safe. But who could I tell this to and for what purpose? I was a lump of clay shaped on the potter's wheel of Allahabad University, and baked in the furnace of Delhi University. They aren't just names of places for people like me, but an integral part of our identity. When this identity is threatened, everything falls apart.

The situation has changed so much that those who previously opposed universities becoming political hubs are now being political in the name of those institutions. In the Union budget, the allocation for education has been steadily decreasing. The attacks on education, institutions and academics are increasing. But the biggest concern now is that people are silent about these attacks, and some are even happy about them.

In Jamia today, the Delhi Police brutally attacked the students who had been studying in the library since morning. The police alleged that the students of Jamia had held demonstrations in support of the CAA, and NRC movements, which had led to violence. They used this excuse to attack the students. During this assault, someone's eye was injured, and someone's hand was broken. Police and paramilitary forces from farmer-worker families were unleashing violence on students also from the same background. The country is watching all this. A few days ago, a similar scene was witnessed at AMU, where tear gas shells were fired inside the campus.

The police can now do anything without the permission of the Vice Chancellor of Jamia. The university campuses of the country have changed drastically. And the citizens of the country are silently watching this change.

That night, the girls of Jamia showed courage, but who cares? We'll smell gunpowder and find pieces of broken glass in Jamia's library for years to come.

The books in the library must have wept that night.

The young men were angry because there were no vacancies.
They started agitating.

16th January 2020

Such Exasperation

I have come to give an interview at Banaras Hindu University. After filling out the form many times, the interview was ultimately scheduled. A few acquaintances came to meet me. As I was passing through the Lanka gate with them, a person came running and angrily said,

"Listen, Laxman, you aren't interested in a career, why are you ruining our chances?"

"Bhai sahab, I do not even know you. How could I harm your career?"

"We have to bear the brunt of the revolution you keep staging. Nobody gives us a job. Everybody says the same thing. That Laxman Yadav has made enough of a mockery of all of us, now we won't let any Yadav into the institution, even by mistake."

"I don't comprehend what you are saying."

"I am also a Yadav. My father registered my name as Gunjan Kumar Yadav. My career is getting ruined because of you."

"Then you should join the Sangh, you will get a job, right?"

"Nothing happened. I am so fed up. I have written posts criticising you from five Facebook accounts, but before the interview, someone shows them my post on social justice. All my hard work goes down the drain. Being a Sanghi is good luck, but to be from a higher caste is to be fortunate. Now, how can I change my caste? I beseech you, bhai, please stop this revolution business. Does anyone from some other community do all this?"

I was moved on hearing all this. A friend from BHU was watching and said, "Don't worry, let's go." Late at night, videos of police entering the rooms of students preparing for competitive exams in Allahabad and beating them with sticks went viral on social media. The young men were angry because there were no vacancies. They started agitating. The UP government was afraid that a student's movement might begin in Allahabad and they sent the police to quell the situation, which they did with their batons and boots, crushing so much else under them.

They have brains too...

16th July 2020

Those who have a head, also have a brain

The result for the posts in the Hindi department of BHU is out today. All the names that were discussed before the interview have been made permanent. Everywhere in the country, universities have become graveyards for the dreams of youth who wish to become professors. What to say of permanent and ad hoc placements, even admission to PhD is determined beforehand nowadays. Every powerful group sends its list. All the candidates of the most powerful person, a few of the less powerful, and one or two candidates of the weakest get selected.

Everyone knows how to get admission to a PhD program and secure a permanent placement. I went to sit in the college staff room. I signalled quietly to Azam who instantly placed green tea in front of me, in my cup. In college, I feel most connected to Azam. He had come from Bihar to work in Delhi. He cares a lot for his wife and children although they live in extreme poverty. Azam, who never gets worried, is a bit restless today. I went to him and asked what was wrong. He said,

"Nothing, sir. My wife is unwell. I need to take her home. Meanwhile, the expenses have significantly increased. I have been asking the staff association to raise the salary for a long time. God knows when they will give me a raise. If you can do something about it, please let me know. Forget that, you are just like us, working on a contract. The government pays your salary, while the staff association pays mine, that is the only difference between us. Never mind."

"Azam, you must have completed ten years here by now and I have been working here for almost fourteen. We have seen so much change. What do you think?"

"Now, it's not like before, sir. Now people don't even speak to each other from the heart. Whatever it is, how does it concern me? I have to keep an account of the tea leaves and sugar and count the cups and plates. It is your responsibility to think and observe, you all are academics. There is a change in the air, for sure."

Just then, Mohammad Zubair from the Urdu department came up to me. Whenever Zubair sir comes, the aroma of khamiri roti wafts in from the direction of the Urdu department. He invites me to eat biryani, I eat khamiri roti. Zubair sir has become a professor and has moved to Jamia. He is connected with me on social media. Whenever we meet, he recites a couplet.

"Laxman, my friend!

jo sar rakhte hain, sar ke bheetar maghaz rakhte hain,
aajkal ve badee mushkil men hain.

Today, when I went to the Campus, a person came to me with a box of sweets at Gate number four and said, "Have some sweets, sir, I am Suresh. I was a guard at Gate No. 4 in this university. We used to meet often, didn't we?"

"Oh, yes, even when we passed by late at night, we would find you studying."

"Yes, sir, my hard work and your blessings have paid off. I have passed the SSC exam. You remember, you had given me a pen one day. I wrote the exam with that very pen."

✿ Those who have heads, have brains too,
These days they are in great trouble too.

Today, the cabinet has approved the New Education Policy.

29th July 2020

29th July 2020

The Seller Sold off the Garden

Today, the cabinet has approved the new education policy. You may not know the entire situation, but let me tell you. At a time when the parliament was not functioning properly and the world was battling COVID, the government took advantage of the situation. It implemented the new National Education Policy 2020 and the farmer and labour laws. Surprisingly, this education policy was implemented without any discussion in the parliament. This is the New India. It is being discussed everywhere. In the college staff room, while drinking tea, Prof. Sandeep Kumar said,

"Why don't you see that Indian languages are being promoted, it has multiple entry and exit options and a multi-discipline and cultural orientation. Why focus only on the drawbacks?"

"But what about issues like the Board of Governors, taking loans from HEFA, 40% online teaching, self-financed courses, what about all that?"

"This is the need of the hour, sir."

The discussion was still going on when Javed Saheb arrived. After his retirement, he comes to the college occasionally. Despite all efforts to the contrary, my college staff room remains amicable. But when Javed Saheb comes, the vibe becomes completely socialist. The room is filled with laughter."

I sat with him again to drink the tea he'd made himself. He recited a couplet:

nasheman hee ke lut jane ka gam hota to kya gam tha,
yahan to bechne wale ne gulshan bech dala hai.

Meanwhile, the day was made for those who turn adversity into opportunity. Someone had opened a shop to publish research papers and became an editor, while another had begun organising seminars and Faculty Development Programs. Ajay often says that Pramod Pandey has earned lakhs of rupees by organising seminars and has three flats in Delhi alone. The UGC's yearly list has not been published in vain. This is just business. To get a paper published costs two thousand rupees. For a one-year-old issue, it is four thousand rupees. For a five-year-old issue, it is five thousand rupees. The fixed rate for future issues is two and a half thousand rupees. Everyone from UGC to the selection committee is aware of all this, but since the world is a stage, everyone is acting.

✪ Loss of a nest, what sorrow would it be?
The seller sold off the garden in entirety

A mirror reflects whoever is in front of it. There are no mirrors that reflect the sadness of all faces.

14th August 2020

Studying without a mobile phone

I have stopped getting newspapers. To stay updated, I just glance through online newspapers in the morning. The first COVID lockdown is about to end. Classes are still being held online. I just saw the news that the education department of the Government of India has released a list of top central universities today. In this, Jamia Millia Islamia ranked first, JNU was second, and Aligarh Muslim University was fourth. Delhi University is not even among the top ten. Today, the Jamia, JNU, and AMU campuses are filled with fresh air. It has been pouring since morning, and even the sick are out for a walk in this changing weather. But, I've got to take a class.

I felt slightly uneasy after the online class today. Only 22 out of 103 students attended. Two dozen students have already called and messaged me saying they do not have smartphones, the internet speed is poor and they cannot join my class. Just then Suresh called and asked-

"After the COVID lockdown, the ad hoc faculty was made to join on August 10, but what about guest lecturers like me? I have not paid my house rent for the past four months. I'm borrowing money to meet basic expenses. I haven't received any payment for the days I taught last semester at the School of Open Learning and Non-Collegiate Women's Education Board. If there's any chance of getting a job, I'll stay, otherwise, I'll have to leave Delhi and return home. My uncle owns a fertiliser and seed store. He says, 'Being a professor is no longer your cup of tea. Come and manage the business. You will not starve.' What shall I do?"

"If I return home, I will never be able to fit into this system again. What should I do, sir? Please guide me." I couldn't decide which was more painful, that Sushma could not attend online classes or that Suresh, who completed his PhD two years ago, had no job. This is the reality of our higher education system today. A mirror reflects whoever is in front of it. There are no mirrors that reflect the sadness of all faces.

SHE faced a lot of injustice and humiliation, but SHE didn't get scared or back down.

September 2023

Cowdung, Cowshed and Nitu Singh's agitation

The Delhi University has changed completely. DUTA has also changed. This year, the biggest change happened in my own college. After several ad hoc principals, Maulana Azad Delhi College now has a permanent principal. One day, Mohammad Muzeeb, a retired professor of our college, came to the staff room. During our conversation, he openly expressed his feelings,

"Delhi College is a place close to my heart. Even after retirement, whenever I return, it doesn't feel like the first time. But today, I feel a pang in my heart. Have you ever thought about whether there's a Muslim principal at any other DU college? No, right?

There was one college. They should have left it like that. One can find qualified people from every caste, community, and religion, one of them should have been chosen. They'd have still worked for you. Even though in name, the colour and diversity would have remained. This system is very narrow-minded."

Muzeeb Sahab had retired from the Urdu department. Whenever he came to college, he always met me. After the success of the roster movement, I began writing and speaking openly on various social and political issues. Today, Muzeeb sir embraced me and said,

"Whenever I see you, I feel as if there's still hope. Your words have a purity to them. I don't know what will happen to you in this job because the circumstances have changed drastically. But your future will be bright, my prayers are with you."

Two friends from the Economics department, who happened to be sisters, gave me a lot of encouragement. We would sit together and discuss our dreams and aspirations. We would bring a corner of the staff room to life. Just then, Tauqeer Anwar showed me a social media post about a massive yajna that was being performed in a college on the North Campus. It was the same college where there was a controversy regarding replacing the girls' hostel with a cowshed. The issue had gone viral on social media.

Meanwhile, a strange incident came to light. Dr. Nitu Singh, a psychology professor from a Dalit family, was expelled from the college. Nitu claimed she was also subjected to casteist insults.

Have you ever considered how many principals in DU's almost 90 colleges are Dalit, backward, or tribal? In 100 years of DU, how many vice-chancellors have been non-upper caste? No, right? Whose responsibility is it to think about this issue?

On the one hand, DU is commemorating its 100th anniversary by distributing gold coins, on the other, Dr. Nitu Singh's agitation is taking place. In a speech today, Nitu said,

"Today, DU has completed 100 years. The university has thrown out people like me. The principal humiliated me. The principal accused me saying that my students had complained against me. I filed a case. During the investigation, most of the students were found to be fake. Which means there were no students with those roll numbers in the college. The charge sheet has been filed. I was fired from my job, false allegations were made against me. DUTA tried, but I didn't get justice. Now, a Dalit's daughter will fight for justice. My community will stand with me. We will fight without fear of the repercussions. We don't want a job, we want justice."

Near the place Nitu was holding her protest, Rakesh told us, "Her principal is angry that she had spoken so frankly. She dislikes Ambedkarites because of her right-wing affiliation. Nowadays, who likes people who speak out? See, who is speaking out in DU now? Everyone has either gone silent or joined the other side."

How many girls dare to fight like Dr. Nitu Singh? She protested for months at the DU gate. She faced a lot of injustice and humiliation, but she didn't get scared or back down. A fearlessly fighting Nitu remains a beacon of hope for this lifeless society. Nitu is still fighting with the pen and the Constitution as her weapons.

You are *SLAVES* of those in power.

2023

Another Rohith in DU

Today the results of the interviews, held at Lakhimal College, will be announced. The principal of the college used to work previously in the English department of our college and was rather fearless. The final interviews are being held today and the results will be disclosed around 4 pm.

Them went well. Pandit Gajodhar came from JNU. His interview was just before mine. When he came out, he said, "They asked me how many poets were there in Ashtachhap?"

"Five," I said.

"No, listen to the question carefully. How many poets were there in Ashtachhap?"

"There were five only"

"They got upset and spoke angrily, 'Please leave! You won't be able to do this!' I had hardly reached the door when a board member behind me said,

'How many times did we hint that Ashta means eight? You couldn't even tell that.'

"If I answered eight, would you have made me permanent?"

"What kind of people are you? I have heard that this interview you are conducting is a sham. If my 'setting' works, I will get the job, you won't be able to stop me, and if not, you won't be able to give me anything too. You all are pawns. You are slaves of those in power. One will secure a permanent placement for his daughter and another for his daughter-in-law. The third only wants to become a VC somewhere, so you will all just humiliate us JNU people. In the end, Jagaram Hani's will prevail."

"Look,bhaiya! They're asking the antecedents of a candidate already selected for the position. They're asking me, 'Tell us your father's name."

I said, "You are speaking negatively, sir. It is not like that at all."

"You're completely clueless. This time the Sangh will ensure everything. The monitoring is being done using three filters. First, our communists did it, followed by the Congress. Now that they've got the opportunity, they plan to choose candidates very carefully. They've already promoted the seniors to shut them up; otherwise, the day an investigation is conducted, it'll be evident that people became professors by writing articles consisting of only two paragraphs."

"No, sir, you're just saying anything. If they do not select us, that doesn't imply that everything has been fixed."

"Laxman, I have given twelve interviews in the last six months. I've seen the entire gamut of this problem. Now don't pretend you were unaware that a scam was taking place."

"Oh, come on, sir. That is too much. What proof do you have?"

'There's no evidence either that a temple stood where the mosque used to be. But it's being built at that location itself, right? What did the court say? Public sentiment. So just because there's no proof, it doesn't mean everything is fine. Now listen! One hundred and fifty interviews are conducted in one day. Everything has already been 'settled' from top to bottom. You take care of yourself. I've heard your principal is the Delhi head of the education department. He's been sent there for a specific reason. Take care, bhaiya. I have to warn you, it is my duty."

"If you know everything, why don't you stop giving interviews?' 'Leave it, sir. No one can make sense of these things. People just keep spreading rumours."

"Look at him. He will surely get the job. He didn't get it at Vanshraj College because the Principal madam there wanted to appoint a favourite student. Don't be under any illusion. Be realistic. These campuses are ruined. I want to see the devastation at every level, that's why I will keep coming to give every interview so that when the time comes to kill them all, I can remember each face. By the way, didn't Samarvir die? Who killed him? They'll all die."

Samarvir was an ad hoc professor at Birsamunda College. He wasn't given a permanent position. He was the sole support of his family. He couldn't bear the treachery and the resulting depression. He hanged himself.

When Pandit Gajodhar left for JNU, it was my turn for the interview. It went on for four or five minutes. Let's see who gets the position today. I got a call from Sanjay Kumar at 2 pm. He called from the DUTA office to congratulate me on getting the job at Lakhimal College. I assumed he was joking, so I ignored it, but my mind remained there. At around 7 pm, the phone rang again.

"Hello, Laxman! Congratulations!"

"Thank you, but I'm afraid I don't recognise you, and I don't know why you're congratulating me."

"Hey, I'm Ranjan Kumar, from the college, yaar. Congratulations on getting a permanent position at Lakhimal College!"

"But sir, I haven't received any intimation yet."

"If I have congratulated you, please be sure that nothing can stop you now."

I received a few more calls congratulating me. Later in the night, I learnt I was supposed to get the job, but the news reached the higher-ups, and things got messed up. It was decided that Laxman's name should be removed. This was the first time in history that congratulations were given in vain."

The interviews for permanent positions in the Hindi Department will be held from November 29th.

20th November 2023

Dakshina for becoming a Guru

There were a lot of emails from my college today. One of them was from the selection committee of the Hindi Department. The interviews for permanent positions in the Hindi Department will be held from November 29th. That afternoon, I went to see one of my senior professors. We used to play cricket together. He held me in high regard. I said to him, "Sir, I haven't come to ask you for anything. All I want is your advice about what I should do at this point. This is my college. I won't go anywhere else if I don't get selected here. Whoever I am and whatever I have done so far, all that has been my choice. There's no need to discuss that."

"Look, many of our own people have painted you in a bad light."

"How?"

"They say he's an ideological opponent, he travels all over the country speaking against us, he is always arrogant, everyone has made compromises to get a job but he is so unyielding, he's anti-Sangh, a leftist, will be difficult to keep in control, will cause trouble later. All this. And you already know all this, it's nothing new."

"Then what should I do, sir?"

"What can you do? You've already done everything you shouldn't have done and you are far ahead on that path. Everyone knows you're not in the wrong, otherwise, how would you have survived in this system for 14 years? But look, this is the reality. Whoever is in power will do what he wants. I sincerely hope that you get the placement. All the best."

As I came out, I ran into a retired professor and two or three of my seniors. He was there to get his pension papers made. He has a good relationship with the principal. Raman Kumar sir asked him to look out for the interests of the 'kids', the ad hoc professors. Right away, that man began speaking -

"Oh, no need to worry about him. He's got Lalu and Mulayam to take care of him. Akhilesh Yadav or Tejashwi Yadav will give him a job!"

Yes, this is the mentality of a retired professor who has worked with me. It's not the first time this has happened. I came home, got busy with work, and began waiting for my interview. I didn't go anywhere nor did I tell anyone anything.

Then Sanchit called. He said, "They're removing people selectively. They're removing even those who aren't on the list. They showed me a picture of the roster movement, in which I am with you.

And they turned me down. They said he was Laxman Yadav's friend. I wish I had deleted my social media account like Ramesh did. Then I think, Mahendra Yadav did all that. Still, a 10-year-old photo from JNU surfaced on the day the interview results were announced. I was even offering to pay a 'Dakhsina'. Still, they didn't take me. The scenario is bad, bhaiya. You must be aware of the situation you are in."

My heart seemed to have stopped beating. A bird should not be separated from its tree. However, Time had other plans. The minions of the ruler had prepared well for this moment.

6th December, 2023

The bird flew away

My college announced it formally via an email. I was dismissed from my college after teaching there for almost fourteen years. My heart seemed to have stopped beating. A bird should not be separated from its tree. However, Time had other plans. The minions of the ruler had prepared well for this moment. What I was afraid of, had happened. But when it happened, it made me realise a lot of things.

My interview went well. Since I had done my research on Tulsidas, they asked me a question, at the end of the interview, about 'Taadna'. Understanding the deep political implications of the question, I gave a balanced answer. I could read their eyes. I knew why all this was happening.

On December 3rd, when the result for Hindi Department's permanent positions was finalised, I received a message from a member of the interview board, in the evening - 'I am so sorry, Laxman.' Just these five words. Suddenly, my heart sank. I had been fortifying myself for this moment for a long time, believing that when the moment came, I wouldn't be weak. However...

Ironically, I was in Nagpur that day. I had to speak at a program on Constitution Day. I first called my wife and was unable to say much. I just told her about the five-word message and said, 'This is the message I received.' After saying that I...

I gave fourteen years of my life to that college, and they took it from me. This college shaped a rough twenty-one and a half years old me into what I am today. And I have been asked to leave that very college. There is no such rule and no need was felt to provide a reason for my dismissal. They know everything, and so do I. My only regret is that many people from the college, those I considered close, didn't give me the support I needed.

I was anxious about how my mother and elder uncle would react. My mother said, "I've been saying this since the beginning, be careful. Avoid speaking too much. But neither your father ever listened to me nor have you. Now look, you've been thrown out. Never mind, though. Don't worry, don't be sad. If nothing happens, come home, don't worry. All will be well."

My elder uncle said, 'This sacrifice is small for the battle you are fighting. You're in the right, your struggle is valid. One day, the oppression of these tyrants will end. Don't worry at all. We're here for you.'

The students in my college organised a protest. People started calling to console me. Thousands of calls came. Thousands of people wrote supportive posts on social media. Protests and agitations were organised in hundreds of places. And a memorandum was submitted to the President. You won't believe it, there were dozens of such calls where people were crying over the phone, saying, 'Sir, injustice has been done to you. We're always with you, sir. I just said,

mere lahaje men jee-huzoor na tha,
aur koi mera qasoor na tha.

Two days later, I went to the college to return all the papers and documents. Tauqeer Anwar came to see me off to the car and started crying, saying, 'I don't know what to say.' My students learned I had come to the college, and many gathered around me. Their eyes had tears of pain, and they were angry. I talked to them for a long time. Maybe for the last time. After they left, I sat alone in the car and kept looking at the tree from which had been taken from me.

In the evening, I found out that two of my senior teachers had said, 'You shouldn't bite the hand that feeds you.' 'He wants to speak up and create a ruckus, then he wants a permanent job too.'

All my colleagues got permanent positions, except for me. I decided to raise my voice against this injustice. I demanded to know the reason for my dismissal. Instead of making it a personal fight, I saw it as a part of the deterioration in higher

---

✪ To be servile, didn't have it in me
To no other crime do I plead guilty

education. Many professors from DU supported me, and we held a press conference. One evening, an elderly woman called me.

Crying, she said, "Laxman beta, my daughter was also dismissed after eight years. A person who got a permanent placement said, 'The rate is half for internal candidates. Didn't you try to pay them off?' My daughter has been in depression since then. We have taken her to the hospital. No one cares. After seeing your courage, I called just to bless you. Everyone else has become heartless. I curse these sinners, they will bear the brunt, someday. The old woman hung up, crying. Then I saw that a person, who had obtained a permanent placement, posted a photo of his joining, writing that he is the first professor from Chambal. And that his mother had tears in her eyes.

What a difference there was between the tears of these two mothers!

The fight is still on. Because this fight has been going on before me and will continue after me. What I did was just one phase of a long battle, it has passed. Time alone will tell how I did.

The next day, Mohammad Shakir called me in the morning. He said, "I am going to the college, for the joining....without you. We had arrived at this college together, we kept coming together every day, today I will have to go alone." Then, there was a long silence and the phone was disconnected.

A Professor's Diary